TALES OF GLORY

The Stories Icons Tell

TALES OF GLORY

The Stories Icons Tell

MATTHEW W. GAUL

LEONINE PUBLISHERS
PHOENIX, ARIZONA

Published by Leonine Publishers LLC
PO Box 8099
Phoenix, Arizona 85066
USA

ISBN-13: 978-0-9887729-9-1

Library of Congress Control Number: 2013949908

10 9 8 7 6 5 4 3 2 1

Printed in the United States of America

Visit us online at www.leoninepublishers.com
For more information: info@leoninepublishers.com

This work is dedicated
to the Protection of the Blessed Virgin Mary,
and humbly submitted to the judgment of the Church.

St. Nicholas Ukrainian Greek Catholic Church
Watervliet, NY

Contents

Chapter 1: The Vault and the Sanctuary

Chapter 2: The Iconostasis

Chapter 3: Side Shrines

Chapter 4: Vault Feasts and Scenes

Chapter 5: Wall Feasts and Scenes

Appendices

Acknowledgements

If in the following pages you find anything flawed or blameworthy, lay it squarely at my feet, and impute no fault to the delightful people below.

Thanks to those who encouraged me: Fr. Mikhail Myshchuk, for approaching me several times despite myself; and my wife Karen Gaul, who encouraged me when I was lazy and tolerated the displacement of domestic time and energy which this effort entailed.

Gratitude to those who gave suggestions: notably Fr. Deacon Thomas Gutch, who mentioned that I should cite the Bible for the benefit of Protestants and include a glossary; and Peter Fil, who suggested the calendar organization in the appendix, among several other ideas.

Much appreciation to Peter Fil for layout and all the time spent in meetings, and putting up with my desire to have everything done yesterday and perfectly; to photographer Timothy Raab of Tim Raab Northern Photo; to proofreaders Msgr. John Terlecky, Deacon William Gaul, Alice Gaul, Karen Gaul, and the very thorough editor at Leonine.

A tip of the hat to those people whom I don't know personally but who were kind enough to answer one or more of my unexpected questions—Roman Markovych, Addison Hodges Hart, John Salza, and several members of the ByzCath.org forum.

Praise and glory to Jesus Christ; and honors to Mary, and to my guardian angel, and probably to many others beyond this earthly vale, for inspiring me to buy an icon of St. George—it sat on my desk for years, slowly guiding me in my journey to St. Nicholas Church.

Foreword

Now this is eternal life: That they may know thee, the only true God, and Jesus Christ, whom thou hast sent (Jn 17:3).

To know God and His only-begotten Son, our Lord and God, Jesus Christ, should be the ultimate goal of every believer. To achieve this goal, we must seek help. This help comes from the Church. She has the authority and ability to teach us about God, and she has the experience and knowledge that will lead us to a practical and personal relationship with God.

The Church, as a wise mother, first of all teaches us how to pray, and through this prayer she presents us to God, so that we may know "the only true God, and the one whom [he] sent, Jesus Christ." Jesus is "the image of the invisible God" (Col 1:15)—the One who brings us to the Father through His image, His icon. An icon then is a way into heaven. Indeed, it has been said that an icon is a "window into heaven."

It was to reveal the hidden treasure of Eastern Christianity, and particularly of St. Nicholas Ukrainian Catholic Church, that Matthew Gaul took up the challenge of writing this book about icons. He did this to help the parishioners both know and understand the message of each icon in the church. I am confident that many will find this book interesting and edifying, and I hope that many more will be captivated by the beauty and richness of our Eastern Tradition.

Thanks be to God in the Holy Trinity, now and forever and ever. Amen.

Rev. Mikhail Myshchuk
Pastor, St. Nicholas Church

Preface

When I first arrived at St. Nicholas, I felt hesitant and even unworthy, for the presence of God was so obvious and arresting that I almost did not know how to handle it. It was an honor simply to be let in the door.

The Greek Rite is precisely what had always been missing from my spiritual life, though I did not realize it. I am so grateful for it. I believe that it may very well be the crucial thing missing from the lives of millions—no, billions—of others; unfortunately, so many of those who hunger are seeking in dark places for they know not what.

The overwhelming glory of the Lord shines forth in the beauty of the chant and the icons, in the passionate language of the texts, and in the humble reverence of the kisses and prostrations. This God-oriented yet deeply human worship exists in sublime contradiction to the technocratic and materialist modern world—and is therefore an antidote. Even many of our Catholic brethren who are righteously devoted to the humanity of Christ could benefit from rediscovering an appreciation for the unspeakable might and majesty of the blessed and glorious Trinity.

I beg Our Lord that this effort will in some small way help the Greek Catholic tradition take root and flower on our soil.

I entreat you as well to please pray that Christ will increase His entire Church, especially the Greek Rites and particularly the Ukrainian Catholic Church, to which I owe so much for having revealed to me this radiant jewel—and most specifically St. Nicholas Parish, which in my opinion deserves nothing less than explosive growth and God's choicest blessings.

Matthew W. Gaul

Introduction

Iconography contains many different levels of meaning and subjects for discussion—theology, art appreciation, Bible stories, devotion, liturgy, history, tales of heroism, and so on.

Each icon's entry begins with a basic explanation. After that, liturgical prayers known as "propers" are available. Finally, detailed discussions of the fine points of the icon are included and arranged by topic, so that you may easily find what interests you. If you are only interested in the "high points," or in certain icons, or in the daily propers, great! You can skip the rest and, I hope, enjoy it later. Everything else will be there waiting for you when you want it.

This book is arranged according to the layout of its inspiration: St. Nicholas Ukrainian Greek Catholic Church. Therefore, the icons are grouped into chapters by their locations in the temple and their relative importance. Most Greek Rite temples follow common norms, and despite their variations are still discernable as members of the same family. And so the book aims to bring the reader an appreciation of the entire tradition, through the lens of St. Nicholas Church.

In other words, although you may certainly read this book cover to cover, you may find it equally enriching to leave it on your coffee table and open it as the inspiration strikes you.

Citations for the Douay-Rheims Bible are provided throughout. Occasionally, scriptural quotes are taken from a translation other than the Douay-Rheims, typically for improved readability, and these instances are noted. Liturgical propers, usually troparia and kontakia, also are noted when they are not taken from the primary source, typically because it did not have them. Useful guides to the versions of the Bible and liturgical texts used here can be found in the appendices.

So as not to presumptuously assume the role of sacred-text translator, I have retained the original form of biblical and liturgical quotations, even if they are not consistent with the text of the book—for example, capitalization of divine pronouns, certain spellings, some traditional "sacred English," and the absence of quotation marks.

Chapter 1:
The Vault and the Sanctuary

And He, like the sun, will by the aid of your purified eye show you in Himself the image of the invisible, and in the blessed spectacle of the image you shall behold the unspeakable beauty of the archetype.

-St. Basil the Great
On the Holy Spirit, AD 375

Christ Pantocrator

From the center of the highest point of the vault of the church, the glorious King of All gazes down upon His people. The centrality and largeness of the icon, along with its intimate close-up portraiture, immediately impress upon the worshipper the profound presence of Christ in the church and in the Divine Liturgy.

Pantocrator is a Greek translation of the Hebrew title *El Shaddai*. It literally means "All Powerful," or more loosely, "Ruler of All."

In English translations of the Bible, it is usually interpreted as "Lord Almighty," as when St. Paul writes, "And I will receive you; and I will be a Father to you; and you shall be my sons and daughters, saith the Lord Almighty" (2 Cor 6:18).

The icon as a whole indicates that Our Lord is here to judge us. He is shown with a serious, perhaps stern, expression, and the gesture of His right hand indicates that He is commanding our attention in direct discourse. This authoritative hand is pointing at Himself, as though He is saying, "I am the one to whom you should be paying attention." In His left hand, He holds the Book of Life, which is closed and clasped tight, only to be opened and read on the Day of Judgment, when the dead will be "judged by those things which were written in the books, according to their works" (Apoc 20:12). Now that the book is closed, the time for repentance and conversion is at an end, and whatever was done, is done.

Troparion, Tone II:
Fashioner of all creation, *
You fixed times and seasons by
Your own authority; * bless the
crown of the year, O Lord, with
Your goodness, * preserving our
nation and Your city in peace;
and save us through the prayers
of the Mother of God.

The church ceiling is of a type called a *barrel vault*—one unbroken semicircle from the north side wall to the south side wall. The ceiling of a Greek Rite church, either in this style or in the *dome* style, represents the vault of heaven, and the King's placement on it as the largest and most central icon gives a foretaste of the formidable Ruler of the Universe on the "Day of the Lord" (Is 2:12; 2 Pt 3:10).

Christ

The gold field of the icon indicates that Christ exists in the Light of God—in the eternal, heavenly reality. He is outside of time, in the eternal Now.

Much of the visual language used here to identify Christ will be repeated in most of the representations of Him seen throughout the church.

The garment nearest His body, a type of tunic called a *chiton*, is blood purple to indicate His royalty and divinity and His death for our salvation. It also identifies Him as the Savior who tramples His enemies, with whose blood His apparel is stained (Is 63:2-4).

The Most Holy has a red stripe running down from His shoulder. This is called a *clavus*, and it was originally a badge of office in the Roman Empire. The color red here carries much the same meaning as the blood purple, and in addition it recalls the scarlet cloak that the cruel soldiers used to mock His kingship during His passion (Mt 27:28).

Our Lord's outer garment is a type of cloak called a *himation*. His is blue, a color used to indicate His humanity. The blue himation is over the red-purple chiton, teaching us that the Son of God is first royal and divine but that he put on His humanity for our sake. Also, in the ancient world, cinnabar red and ultramarine were among the most rare and expensive pigments that an artist would use, and consequently they bespoke the high status of the person thus adorned.

Around Christ's head is a golden circle, a *nimbus*—sometimes called a *halo*—that depicts His divine grace radiating forth from Him. Although to our eyes the nimbus is two-dimensional and bounded, it is a stylized way of representing grace diffusing outward in all directions, much like a candle giving light. Christ's nimbus bears special resemblance to the sun, showing that Christ is the true "Sun of Justice" (Mal 4:2), unlike the false pagan deities and worldly rulers that pretend to this title.

Holy personages are typically adorned with a nimbus, yet Christ has a style particular to Himself—a *cruciform nimbus*, with three arms of His cross visible. These represent the Three Persons of the Trinity, thus identifying Christ as God and indicating that the life of the Father and the Holy Spirit also subsist in Him. Inside the arms are the Greek initials ό ὦ N, which stand for "He Who Is." This is a form of the Divine Name given to Moses, transliterated from the Hebrew *YHWH*, "I AM WHO AM" (Ex 3:14).

Christ almost always has a traditional Greek monogram to emphasize His identity, and this icon is no exception. This style corresponds to our use of initials, but in a different format. The monogram includes the first and last letters of a name, and instead of noting an abbreviation with a period, as we do, it uses an overline.

Christ's monogram is therefore $\overline{\text{IC}}$ $\overline{\text{XC}}$, from the Greek Ἰησοῦς Χριστός, *Iesus Christos*, Jesus Christ.

It is important to note that "Christ" is not His last name but rather His title, being the Greek translation of the Hebrew word "messiah," that is, "Anointed One," who was promised by God to save His people from the evil one (Hb 3:13) and reign over God's empire (1 Kgs 2:10).

Angels

Angels, as is common in iconography, are not represented as they actually are in reality—it would not be possible for man to do so—but rather are conveyed in a symbolic manner to give the viewer an idea of what they are.

Unlike human beings, who are composed of body and soul, angels exist entirely in spirit, and therefore they do not have a material form that of its own nature presents any image to the physical eye, unless God chooses to make them visually present to us (Tb 12:18-19).

The artists of the iconographic tradition have devised a visual language that renders visible the invisible realities of the supernatural realm. Angels are presented as genderless youths—young because they exist in the eternal Now of heaven and genderless because they are neither male nor female.

The spirits are given wings to show us that they descend from a higher place in order to be with us here on earth. Although where they come from is not physically "up"—that is, somewhere to which we could fly—the wings communicate that their place of origin is a reality that is superior to our own.

Angels wear their hair in an elegant curled style that was fashionable in the Late Antique period of the Roman Empire, and their hair is bound by a *fillet*, a band of fabric that was worn by unmarried women of the day. The fillet shows that angels do not give themselves in marriage (Mt 22:30) and that they are free from all the bodily passions with which human beings currently wrestle.

The colors of their dress, as is typical with angels, do not have a specific meaning; they were chosen simply to visually balance the image.

Note also that in the icon these glorious heavenly beings are much smaller than Christ—indeed, their entire bodies are nary as large as the bust of Our Lord. This is a technique known as *hierarchical perspective*, in which the persons or things of greater importance or dignity are larger than other figures in the image.

Troparion, Tone VIII:
When the bodiless angel
learned the secret command *
he hastened and stood before
the house of Joseph * and said
to her who had not known
wedlock, * "The One who
has bowed the heavens by
His condescension * is wholly
contained in you without
change. * In your womb I see
Him taking the form of a slave.
* Therefore I cry to you in
fearful awe: * Rejoice, O Bride
and Virgin!"

Mother of God Platytera (Ton Ouranon)

This icon's Greek name, *Platytera Ton Ouranon*, means "more spacious than the heavens." Because it held the infinite Lord and Creator of all things—which not even the heavenly paradise can do—Mary's womb became figuratively "more spacious than the heavens."

Solomon, after building the glorious Temple for the Lord, marveled at the infinitude of the Divinity and asked, "Is it credible then that God should dwell with men on the earth? If heaven and the heavens of heavens do not contain thee, how much less this house, which I have built?" (2 Par 6:18). But indeed, the fullness of the eternal Creator dwelt within the Mother of God.

The icon is also sometimes called "the Virgin of the Sign" in reference to a prophecy of Isaias: "Therefore the Lord himself shall give you a sign. Behold a virgin shall conceive, and bear a son, and his name shall be called Emmanuel" (Is 7:14).

The Virgin stands in the traditional *orans* prayer position—hands outstretched, offering her supplications to God on our behalf. Christ is shown in a medallion that is her womb. The archangels Gabriel (to the viewer's left) and Michael bow to them, and in turn the Blessed Lady intercedes for us with Our Lord and guards the Divine Liturgy and the church from their enemies.

The first and last letter of the Greek alphabet, A and Ω (alpha and omega), are monogrammed to left and right, for the Lord God refers to Himself in Scripture as "the Alpha and the Omega"—in other words, the beginning and end of all things, the source of all and the final destination of all (Apoc 1:8, 21:6, 22:13).

Above, the Holy Spirit in the form of a dove descends upon the Virgin to effect the conception of Our Lord. He wears a cruciform nimbus typical of Christ, reminding us that the entire Trinity is present with Him.

Our blessed and glorious Lady is right in the front of the church—in the *apse*, that is, the half-dome recess above the sanctuary—overlooking the Eucharistic miracle and leading us to God. Gabriel and Michael, as representatives of the vast celestial choir, remind us that all those holy and noble beings are as truly present during the liturgy as the person sitting in the next pew; indeed, they ceaselessly join in our prayers and give them great efficacy.

Our Lord and Lady

The King and Queen of heaven (Apoc 12:1-5) are depicted on a larger scale than the angels, in accordance with hierarchical perspective, to emphasize their greatness. They are also raised upon a highly ornate platform as a sign of status; the angels are also on platforms, but the size and adornment of the central platform convey the special importance of the central figures.

The Virgin wears a long red veil, called a *maphorion*, over a blue chiton. Notice that this is the reverse of Christ—the blue representing her humanity is closer to her body, that is, her original nature, but she was clothed by God with His divinity. The three stars on her maphorion represent her perpetual virginity before, during, and after giving birth to Our Lord.

Her hair does not show through—it is bound by a type of coif called a *kekryphalos*, a snug covering once worn by women of Greece, Syria, and other areas of the Near East. It is used in iconography to show that the lady pictured is married.

Mary wears red slippers, the traditional footwear of Eastern Roman emperors and empresses. The iconographers could do no less than show the Queen in attire befitting her status. She is royal, yet tucked into her belt is a white cloth—for she is the handmaiden of God, ever ready to serve Him and work according to His will.

She is monogrammed M͞Р Θ͞Y, from the Greek for "Mother of God"—*Μητηρ Θεου, Meter Theou.*

Christ blesses the assembly, as is evident in the depiction of His hand. The fingers form the IC XC monogram: index finger straight, creating the "I," then the middle finger bent to create a "C," then the ring finger and thumb crossed as an "X," and lastly the pinky curved into a second "C." This is a standard gesture of blessing used in iconography, and it is also the hand position used by priests when they give blessings.

In Christ's left hand is a *rotulus*, an early type of scroll that was used for holding vast amounts of information, and thus it symbolically asserts that He is Wisdom itself, the Incarnate Logos, the Word of God. The rotulus is closed, showing us that He knows more of the divine mysteries than we could ever possibly learn through all eternity.

Although Christ is still in the womb, he is shown more as a small young adult—not a boy or a baby, and certainly not a preborn baby. To show Christ as a baby would imply that He was a typical human child, which of course He was not.

Troparion, Tone IV:
Princes of the heavenly host,
* we, though unworthy, * beg
you to encircle us through your
prayers * under the shelter
of the wings of your spiritual
glory. * Guard us as we come
to you * and sincerely cry:
"Deliver us from dangers, O
princes of the powers on high!"

Rather, He is depicted in a way that shows how He was already fully developed in wisdom and grace, even though His physical body was still very young.

The Lord wears white and gold in this icon, not His typical red or purple with blue. Visually, this helps the viewer's eye to not lose Him amidst the larger red and blue field of His mother. White and gold are often used for Christ in Majesty, as the High Priest and King, or during the Transfiguration; thus, if for practical reasons His normal palette is not ideal, these two colors are a good alternative. White and gold hues shine forth His radiance, and gold was the color of the buckles and girdles worn by Israelites of royal blood (1 Mc 10:89; Dn 10:5; Apoc 1:13).

The Blessed Mother and Child are shown in a blue, almond-shaped area called a *mandorla*—a kind of full-body nimbus that portrays the heavenly realm breaking into our world and the exceptional brilliance of the divine life within those enclosed (Apoc 22:16); the divine light is so intense that it must radiate outward in all directions. Christ's inset medallion is also done in the form of a mandorla.

Christ Emmanuel

Most iconographic depictions of the Lord as a small child are generically referred to as *Christ Emmanuel*, or simply *Emmanuel*. This Hebrew title translates to "God With Us." Originating in the aforementioned prophecy of Isaias, it emphasizes the sublime novelty of the Incarnation and is a fitting epithet for the young Jesus.

The Heavens

Twelve stars dot the field around the outer rim, likely a reference to Apocalypse 12:1: "And a great sign appeared in heaven: A woman clothed with the sun, and the moon under her feet, and on her head a crown of twelve stars." The woman in the verse is mystically understood to be both the Church of Christ and, in another sense, the Mother of God, and thus the twelve stars are a fitting decoration for both her and the Church.

Gabriel and Michael

These two members of the heavenly host have always been dear to the Church, and rightly so, for they ceaselessly work on our behalf. Gabriel came to the aid of the prophet Daniel (Dn 8:16, 9:21), proclaimed the birth of John the Forerunner to his father Zacharias (Lk 1:19), and most gloriously announced the conception of Our Lord to Mary (Lk 1:26).

Michael is honored throughout all of Christendom as the special angelic defender of God's people, the great prince (Dn 12:1) who buried Moses (Jude 1:9) and who fights the dragon that is our evil enemy (Apoc 12:7).

Much of the visual language of the iconographic tradition was formed during Late Antiquity, in and around the Byzantine, or more properly, the Eastern Roman Empire. Thus, the visual language uses concepts and items that communicated ideas that were readily understood by the reasonably educated people of the day. The angels, for instance, wear the clothes of imperial officials and court chamberlains in Constantinople—they attend to the Emperor of the universe and His affairs, just as the courtiers in Constantinople attended to the human emperor.

They wear a jeweled *dalmatic*, a type of tunic once worn by the upper classes of Byzantine society that eventually evolved into a purely liturgical garment. Around their necks are decorative imperial mantles known as *superhumerals*.

Our angels have donned special jeweled slippers called *buskins*. Eastern Roman emperors wore purple buskins, and various types became common liturgical garments during the first millennium. They are no longer in common use.

Although traditionally the colors of an angel's wardrobe are chosen for visual balance, we can surmise that here, above the Eucharistic Sacrifice, the artist chose to give them red dalmatics to represent their close connection to the divine life.

Notice how the tie-ends of the fillets float behind their ears, indicating that they are ever attentive to the commands of God. Michael and Gabriel both carry a staff in the hand nearer to us; this is an ancient symbol of the office of messenger. Indeed, our word "angel" comes to us through Latin from the Greek word for "messenger," ἄγγελος, *angelos*. The proper name for the staff they carry as angels is *merilo*, which literally means a "measure."

In their other hands they each carry a *globus*, a symbol of their dominion, and the chi-rho inscribed therein shows that they draw this power from Christ. The globus does not simply signify the earth but is instead a representation of the entire celestial sphere of Creation. Thus, the angels hold in their hands a degree of God-given authority over all Creation, and as such they are powerful intercessors on our behalf.

Their names are inscribed in Greek majuscule, each beginning with the monogram for archangel, $\overline{\text{APX}}$, followed by ΓΑΒΡΗΪΛ for Gabriel and MHXAΪΛ for Michael. Gabriel's name is from the Hebrew for "God is my strength," and Michael's name means "He who is like God."

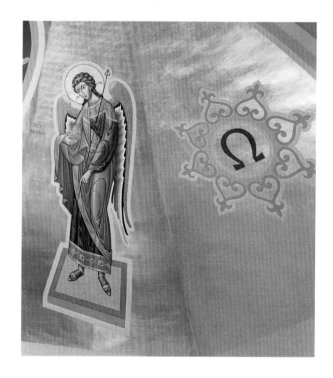

Four Evangelists

Evangelists of the Synoptic Gospels

The accounts written by Matthew, Mark, and Luke are called the *synoptic* Gospels because they share much the same content and chronology. The iconography of these evangelists reflects this by using a consistent style of composition that is not used for St. John. All three are pictured amidst buildings and shown writing their own Gospels, whereas John is shown in a remote location dictating his Gospel rather than writing it, and he faces in the opposite direction from the others.

Mark and Luke both bend an ear to heaven, listening to divine inspirations, for they did not personally witness Christ's earthly ministry. Their icons also show them referencing other scrolls while writing their gospels; these scrolls symbolize the oral tradition they received from their teachers.

Matthew, however, as one of the Twelve Apostles, does not need to rely on the oral tradition and is not shown bent over source material. His head is turned slightly, indicating that he is listening more directly to the whisperings of the Holy Spirit. Tradition holds that he was an older man at the time of his calling.

They are monogrammed in Ukrainian, "СВ. ЄВ.," that is, "Holy Evangelist," followed by their names—МАТВІЙ, МАРКО, ЛУКА, and ІВАН. For those not familiar with the Greek and Cyrillic alphabets, a hint that this is not Greek is that the initials use periods instead of the Ancient Greek–style overlines.

The scrolls of the evangelists typically contain the first verses of their respective Gospels. Yet because these images were not intended for close viewing, the writing on the scrolls does not contain legible words. They would normally read as follows:

Matthew - "The book of the generation of Jesus Christ, the son of David, the son of Abraham" (Mt 1:1).

Mark - "The beginning of the gospel of Jesus Christ, the Son of God" (Mk 1:1).

Luke - "Forasmuch as many have taken in hand to set forth in order a narration of the things that have been accomplished among us" (Lk 1:1).

John the Theologian

John is shown in the desert, seated amidst rocky outcroppings. These stones are interpreted to be either bowing to the beloved disciple or leaping and crying out to God with joy and praise (Lk 19:40). More literally, the scene is the Greek island of Patmos, whither John was exiled by the Roman Emperor Domitian after the ruler boiled the evangelist in oil yet failed to cause him any harm.

A long, deep-blue himation envelops almost his entire body.

John's large, lined forehead symbolizes his profound wisdom. His posture—that is, turned distinctly outward—indicates the depths to which he communicates with God, whom he heard as "a great voice, as of a trumpet" (Apoc 1:10).

John holds a scroll in his left hand, and with his right hand he makes a gesture of discourse to the scribe to whom he is dictating. This youth is Prochorus, one of the seven deacons mentioned in the Acts of the Apostles; according to tradition, he was the nephew of St. Stephen and a companion of the evangelist.

The text on the book would normally read, "In the beginning was the Word, and the Word was with God, and the Word was God" (Jn 1:1).

Feast Day - November 16:
Holy Apostle
and Evangelist Matthew

Troparion, Tone III:
O Matthew, proclaimer of
God's word, * you earnestly
turned from the tax collector's
booth * and followed the
Master, Who out of His love
* appeared to us on earth and
summoned you. * You shone to
the world as chosen apostle and
loud herald of the Good News.
* Because of this we feast your
memory; * pray to God all-
merciful * for the forgiveness
of sins.

Feast Day - April 25:
Holy Apostle
and Evangelist Mark

Troparion, Tone III:
Learning from Peter the chief
apostle * you too became an
apostle of Christ, * and shone
on various lands like the sun.
* O bless'd one, adornment of
Alexandrians, * through you
Egypt was freed from deceit.
* For you are a pillar of light
for the Church * enlightening
all with your teaching of the
Good News. * Therefore, we
feast your memorial, O Mark
divinely inspired. * Ask God
Whom you preached to all * to
grant our souls forgiveness of
sins.

Feast Day - October 18:
Holy Apostle and Evangelist
Luke

Troparion, Tone V:
Let us praise in sacred hymns
the celebrated Luke, * herald
of the acts of the apostles, *
brightly shining author of the
Good News of Christ, * scribe
of things unwritten, which he
wrote for Christ's Church. * He
is a physician for the feeble, *
healing nature's ailments and
the maladies of souls, * and he
prays unceasingly for all of us.

Feast Day - May 8:
Holy Apostle and Evangelist
John the Theologian

Troparion, Tone II:
O beloved apostle of Christ our
God, * hasten, deliver a people
without defense. * He Who
received you when you leaned
upon His breast * accepts you
as you bow in prayer. * Implore
Him, O Theologian, * to
scatter the cloud of nations that
besets us, * asking peace and
great mercy for us.

The placement of elements in the icon conveys an increase in grace and wisdom from the lower right to the upper left: from the cave of darkness, that is, the old life of sin and death; to Prochorus the student; to John the teacher; to God the Master, not visible here. In many icons of this type He is represented as a hand or a ray from the heavens stretching out to the Apostle.

In the background, a small tree with one branch protrudes from the rock. This recalls the prophecy of Isaias: "There shall come forth a rod out of the root of Jesse, and a flower shall rise up out of his root" (Is 11:1). Jesse was the father of King David. The Messiah was expected to come from the lineage of David, but by the time of Jesus' birth, the Davidic line had been absent from the royal house of Israel for hundreds of years. The branch (or rod) shoots from the stump (or root) of the remnants of the royal line, now cut down and humbled. The rod itself is held to be the Mother of God, from David's line, and the flower from the rod is Christ Our Lord.

Other Details

Although the church has a vault ceiling, the images of the evangelists are painted where the *pendentives* would be in a domed church. Architecturally, the pendentives hold up the weight of the dome, and thus the placement of the evangelists reminds us that they support the weight of the Church.

The evangelists do not wear the common raiment of Hebrew fishermen; rather, they are clothed in the elegant dress and hairstyles of upper-class Roman citizens. This noble appearance speaks to their true dignity. All four are clothed in blue or purple himatia; the purple-blue spectrum is often used to indicate the exalted status of the Apostles and evangelists.

Prochorus the deacon is shown in orange-red; this does not necessarily indicate the divine life as it does in other icons, but instead it visually distinguishes him from the loftier blue-purple of the evangelists. The young man is shown in hierarchical perspective, that is, smaller than John.

The swag of red fabric hanging from between two buildings above Matthew, Mark, and Luke is *visual shorthand* to indicate that the events in the icon are taking place indoors. Icons are rarely painted so as to portray an indoor scene because this prevents the use of the gold field, which represents the divine light and is an indispensable element in portraying holy personages.

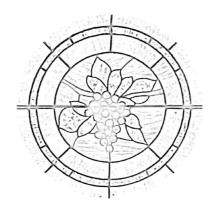

Chapter 2:
The Iconostasis

And you, O most divine and sacred sacrament:
Lift up the symbolic garments of enigmas which surround you.
Show yourself clearly to our gaze.
Fill the eyes of our mind with a unifying and unveiled light.

~St. Dionysius the Areopagite
The Ecclesiastical Hierarchy

Iconostasis

The *iconostasis*, or icon screen, is the large, richly decorated partial wall in the front of the church.

The archetype for the iconostasis is the veil in the Temple of Jerusalem that set apart the most sacred room, the Holy of Holies, from the rest of the structure. The Ark of the Covenant was housed in the Holy of Holies, and God truly dwelt therein. Only the high priest could enter this most sacred place, and even he could enter only once per year on the Day of Atonement, to offer sacrifice to God (Lv 16). In all this we are forcibly reminded that God and man were separate, no longer enjoying the intimate friendship they shared in Eden.

But when the perfect sacrifice of Christ was completed, the Temple veil was rent in two (Mt 27:51; Mk 15:38). This event teaches us, among other things, that all of us may now enter into God's glory and commune with the Most Holy Trinity. Thus, the iconostasis does not completely seal off the sanctuary of the church; rather, it is open, reminding us that the separation between God and man that existed from Adam throughout the Old Covenant has come to an end.

The central doorway—the two *Royal Doors* directly in front of the altar—symbolize the rent Temple veil; indeed, there is usually a parted curtain behind the doors that recalls the veil even more explicitly. When the Royal Doors are open during the liturgy, we have extraordinary access to God.

The Royal Doors are so called because the Eucharistic elements, which will soon become the King of Kings and Lord of Lords (1 Tm 6:15), pass through them during the Great Entrance, just as Christ Himself made His royal entrance into Jerusalem (Mt 21; Lk 19), and this entrance in turn foreshadows His glorious arrival into the New Jerusalem—heaven—after His Resurrection.

To both ends of the screen are the *deacon's doors*, so named because the clergy—usually the deacon—and the acolytes have access to the sanctuary through them.

One could say that the iconostasis does not so much divide the sanctuary from the nave, where the congregation resides, as it does join them together—just as Our Lord brought together heaven and earth. The icon screen thus signifies Christ. As Paul says, "We have confidence to enter the Holies in virtue of the blood of Christ, a new and living way which he inaugurated for us through the veil (that is, his flesh)" (Heb 10:19-20 *CV*).

The Icons

In a semicircle around the sanctuary are placed several kings and prophets of the Old Covenant; these men governed and guided the church of God before the time of Christ (Dt 23:1-8; Ps 21), and therefore they are our fathers in faith. They are usually on an upper tier of the iconostasis, but there was no space to do so in St. Nicholas Church, so they were placed here. These glorious ancients should still be considered part of the "cloud of witnesses" (Heb 12:1) represented on the iconostasis.

Iconostases are always crowned on the top with a cross, and because the great figures of the Old Testament shown here are in a certain sense part of our iconostasis, a cross adorns the highest portion of the arc on which they are painted.

The holy multitude on the iconostasis—the Mother of God, Saints Michael and Stephen, the Apostles and evangelists, and pre-Christian figures—adore the blessed and glorious Trinity made present on the altar in the person of Christ during the Divine Liturgy.

Kontakion, Tone IV:
By Your own choice, O Christ
our God, * You were lifted on
the cross. * Grant Your mercies
to Your new community that
bears Your Name. * By Your
power gladden the faithful
people * and grant them
victory against enemies. *
May they have the help of
Your instrument of peace, the
invincible sign of victory.[1]

The Eucharist

As we approach the iconostasis for the most precious gift of the Holy Mystery of the Eucharist, we see that it is subtly embellished with harmonious motifs, the most prevalent of which are the grape vines that wind their way around the icons and call to mind the wine that is mystically changed into Our Lord's blood during the Divine Liturgy.

Small sheaves of wheat rise from the peaks of the icons and seem to almost crown their subjects. They remind us of the ingredients used in the bread that will becomes our Mystical Food, and they also indicate that the saints thus crowned are among the "wheat gathered into his barn"; they bid us to join them, lest we be among "the chaff he will burn with unquenchable fire" (Mt 3:12).

Crosses on Globes

Atop both Royal Doors and the iconostasis as a whole are crosses on orbs, *globus crucigers*. The globus is not merely the earth but rather the entire celestial sphere, that is, all of Creation with the earth at its center (Gn 1). The cross surmounts the orb as Christ our God presides over all Creation, and thus the globus crucigers proclaim His lordship over all things.

These two crosses, together with the one painted above, create a column of three crosses on the iconostasis, providing an interesting, though perhaps unintentional, Trinitarian allusion.

Christ the Teacher

The Wisdom of God (1 Cor 1:24) stands holding open the Book of Life, upon which is inscribed the Alpha and Omega. He raises His hand to us in blessing.

An icon of Christ is always placed to the viewer's right of the Royal Doors.

Garments

Christ here is attired in a prominent, richly embroidered gold clavus.

He also wears sandals with peculiarly thin, wispy straps. When the iconographers of more northern climates began to learn from their Mediterranean forebears, many of them had little experience with the footwear of warmer regions, and consequently they represented sandals in a stylized and somewhat unrealistic way. This quirk became traditional in the iconographies of many non-Greek cultures, and it endures to this day.

[1] Older translations, apparently more literal, use the more evocative, "May she have as Thy help the invincible trophy, the weapon of peace" (*HT*), or a similar wording (*SB*).

The Sunday of Orthodoxy -
First Sunday of Great Lent

Troparion, Tone II:
We bow before Your most pure image, O kind Lord, * and beg pardon for our sins, O Christ our God. * Of Your own will You consented to ascend the Cross in the flesh * to free Your handiwork from enslavement to the enemy. * In thanksgiving we cry aloud to You: * By coming to save the world, our Savior, You filled all things with joy.

The Book of Life

The tome He holds has two meanings: First, it is the record containing all the human beings who will be saved (Apoc 13:8), and from this originates the name "Book of Life." Second, the Greek letters show us what we need to be saved—that is, the Alpha and Omega, Christ, who is the first and the last, the beginning and the end. He is the Way that leads to salvation (Jn 14:6).

Here the book is open, in contrast to the closed Book of Life from *Christ Pantocrator*. This conveys that while man has Christ as his teacher, he can still strive to have his name inscribed among the elect, but when Christ returns as the Just Judge, what is done is done.

Unique Features

There are a few curiosities in this icon. Christ's nimbus is not cruciform—it lacks the cross behind His head—and instead has embossed rays of light; this is a beautiful but unusual artistic decision.

The coloration of His garments is also reversed from the norm. Typically, the chiton, closer to His body, is red, and the outer himation is blue.

Christ the Rabbi and Holy Tradition

The Jewish *rabbi*, or master, taught by oral tradition to a group of followers who were expected to pass on that tradition, and Our Lord was no exception to this (Lk 10:16; 2 Tm 2:2). The New Testament is replete with exhortations to pass on what is heard, to preach and to hear—indeed, when the Holy Spirit descended on the Apostles, He came with the *sound* of the wind and appeared as *tongues* of fire (Acts 2:2-3).

That Christ is a teacher and carried out His preaching on earth as a rabbi (Mk 11:21) has important consequences for Sacred Tradition.

The Catholic Church has three great means of preserving the Faith: the Holy Scriptures; her divinely instituted teaching authority, or *magisterium*; and the handing on of tradition, or *paradosis*. Nowhere does the Holy Bible say of itself that it, the *written* authority, is the *only* authority. Rather, in numerous instances it gives priority to preaching and verbal instruction (Acts 8:30-3; Heb 5:12; 1 Cor 11:2; et al.).

The Church knows that, in addition to what is recorded in Sacred Scripture, "There are also many other things which Jesus did; which, if they were written every one, the world itself, I think, would not be able to contain the books that should be written" (Jn 21:25). And Christ, to whom all power is given and who promised that He would be with the Apostles until the end of the world, charged them to teach *all things whatsoever* He had commanded (Mt 28:18-20)—He by no means limited this teaching to those things recorded in Scripture. Thus, the Apostles taught their students, who in turn passed these glorious doctrines to the next generation of Christians (2 Tm 4).

Christ, through His Church, continues to be our Teacher, and so it will be until the end of the world (Mt 16:18, 28:19-20).

Mother of God Hodegetria

The title of this icon means, in Greek, "She Who Shows the Way."

The small-adult Christ Emmanuel looks lovingly at His Blessed Mother, holds His rotulus in His right hand, and makes the gesture of teaching to her, perhaps saying, as He did to His Apostles, "I am the way, and the truth, and the life. No man cometh to the Father, but by me" (Jn 14:6).

Our Lady stands, her loving gaze intently focused on the viewer, her right hand pointing decidedly to Christ, whom she recognizes as the only path to salvation. The Virgin Most Merciful implores us to listen to her divine Child, just as she does.

The action of the icon moves from the Son of God, to Mary upon whom He gazes, to the worshipper, for Mary is looking at us. This dynamic teaches us that in the Christian's search for Christ, His blessed and glorious Mother—who holds His attention so deeply and whom He loves so thoroughly—will be an excellent guide on the journey. What Christ has taught to Mary, she will teach to us.

Behind the Royal Doors, Jesus Christ, the Way to heaven, makes Himself present at every liturgy, and thus an icon of Mary is always placed to the viewer's left of the doors—a most pure sign directing us to the sublime mystery of the altar.

Garments

The Son of Man (Mt 12:8) is again not in typical colors so that He is not washed out amidst the red and blue of His mother. The iconographer turns instead to pigments used in other depictions of Our Lord. Orange is a common choice for Christ in Glory after the Resurrection, as it suggests a blazing fire and His intensely radiant splendor. It is also the opposite of blue on the color spectrum, and thus it adds contrast and visual interest.

The Son of the Most High (Lk 1:32) has a section of green fabric on His chiton and Ukrainian-style green embroidery around His neck. Green is the color of life (especially new life), fruitfulness (Gn 1:12), and the regeneration of that which was dead (Jb 14:7). These verdant flashes provide the color that is contrary to the red of the Ever-Virgin's maphorion.

The First Icon

Numerous pious traditions state that St. Luke painted the first icon, and many of these indicate that his work was the first formulation of the *Mother of God Hodegetria*. This theory may be literally true or it may descend from pious reflection on Luke's Gospel, which gives more information than the others about the life of the Holy Family and thus is, in a figurative sense, the first portrait of Christ and His mother.

The Synaxis of the All-Holy Mother of God - December 26

Kontakion, Tone VI:
He Who existed before the morning star * and was born of the Father without a mother, * today, O Full of Grace, becomes flesh from you without a father. * Wherefore, a star brings the news to the Magi * and angels with shepherds sing of how you gave birth ineffably.

The Mystical Supper

Feast Day:
Great and Holy Thursday

Christ celebrates the Pasch with His Apostles, and during this sacred meal he foretells that one of them will betray Him. They all gesture in disbelief and turn to each other to murmur their bewilderment. The emotional Peter, to Christ's right, throws his arms wide and insists upon knowing who it is that will commit this heinous deed.

Irmos, Tone VI:
Come, you faithful, let us lift up our minds on high, * and enjoy the Master's hospitality, * and the Table of Immortal Life in the upper room; * and let us hear and learn the exalted teaching * of the Word, Whom we magnify.

Our Lord replies, "But yet behold, the hand of him that betrayeth me is with me on the table" (Lk 22:21). At this moment, Judas reaches out to dip his hand with Christ.

Thence Our Lord institutes the Eucharistic Sacrifice:

> And whilst they were at supper, Jesus took bread, and blessed, and broke: and gave to his disciples, and said: Take ye, and eat. This is my body. And taking the chalice, he gave thanks, and gave to them, saying: Drink ye all of this. For this is my blood of the new testament, which shall be shed for many unto remission of sins (Mt 26:26-28).

Eucharistic loaves and wine vessels pepper the table.

The disciple beloved by Christ, John the Theologian, leans in close to the bosom of his Master (Jn 13:23), demonstrating that he drank deeply of the sacred mysteries and reached sublime heights of mystical understanding.

This icon is placed prominently over the Royal Doors, beyond which the Eucharistic Sacrifice takes place. This reminds us that the sacrifice of Calvary is truly offered here in the sanctuary, just as Christ mystically anticipated this sacrifice by offering up His Body and Blood during the Mystical Supper.

Temple of Jerusalem

The viewer knows that the action occurs in Jerusalem because of the city wall in the background and the Temple of Jerusalem on our left. This again is visual shorthand, not an exact representation of the elaborate Temple; indeed, diverse representations of the Temple are used by different iconographers in various cultures, but in this case we can recognize the Temple from the tall, thin, rounded entrance under a three-tiered, pointed roof.

Although this scene takes place indoors, there is no swag of hanging fabric here, presumably because the strong horizontality of the icon made its inclusion difficult.

Judas

Judas is reaching noticeably out of his place, representing the pride or greed that impels him to exceed the limits of propriety and obedience. His head is the lowest of all the persons represented, indicating his inferiority through hierarchical perspective, not of scale but of height.

As an act of mercy to the viewer, much of Judas' face is not visible. Because an icon is a window into heaven, when we prayerfully consider the image it helps us to make a true connection with the person represented. Thus, evil people and devils are traditionally shown in profile so that we cannot make eye contact with them, and thus we cannot establish a connection that we wouldn't wish to have.

Judas' garments are orange and green, the exact opposite shades of the red and blue used for Christ's clothing. The purpose of the contrast here is different from that in *Mother of God Hodegetria*. In this case, besides their dark, earthy tones, the orange and green have no meaning of themselves; they merely provide visual contrast between Christ and Judas—the holy Betrayed and the despicable betrayer.

The Other Apostles

There does tend to be some fluidity in the characteristics of many of the Apostles, oftentimes even in works of the same iconographer. But most here conform to common depictions.

Several of them wear visible clavi stripes, signifying their grand offices given by God. Peter the Rock and head of the apostolic college (Mt 16:18-19), Matthew the Evangelist, and perhaps James of Zebedee and Thomas bear these stripes on their arms. Most likely, it was artistic concerns that determined which guests received a clavus.

Peter wears a golden yellow himation, a garment in which he is frequently seen; it underscores his status as the preeminent Prince of the Apostles (Mt 16; 1 Cor 15:4-8; Acts 1:15; et al.). He is also centrally seated, to Christ's immediate right.

The boyish Thomas and Philip are both beardless youths, and it can be difficult to tell them apart.

Amongst the older set, Simon the Zealot is known by his bald head and white rounded beard. Andrew and Matthew are also advanced in years, but they usually have full heads of hair. Andrew can perhaps be discerned by his hair, which is more curly or possibly more haggard than Matthew's.

James of Alphaeus is a man in the prime of his life, with the most pointy beard of the group. Next, Jude and James of Zebedee can be identified by the process of elimination, and by Jude's grayer hair or more worn visage.

Saint Michael the Archangel

The great defender of God's people—the church of old under the Mosaic Law (Jo 5:13-15) and now the Church of Christ—is St. Michael. He bows his head toward the Eucharistic Lord in the sanctuary and bids the worshipper to direct his attention there.

Michael is situated on the north door of the iconostasis, protecting the table behind him, the *prothesis*, where the bread and wine are prepared before the Divine Liturgy.

Garments and Globus

Michael is here rendered somewhat differently than he is in the apse. His previous appearance was courtly and bejeweled, but here he wears the apparel of a soldier, far from home and ready for action.

The fillet tie-ends cupped behind his ears represent his eagerness to listen to God.

His cloak is different from those of most figures—it is a *chlamys*, which is fastened about the neck to allow better access to his sword (not shown) and which can be quickly wrapped around the arm as a light shield. Michael is ready to defend the People of God from the Adversary at a moment's notice.

The celestial being here replaces his formal jeweled buskins with simpler leather ones—more appropriate footwear for fighting.

Our heavenly protector also wears a green *lacerna*, a short, thick, woolen cloak draped over the chiton that was originally used by the Roman military when on campaign outside of Rome. The first lacernae were thought to be inelegant and un-Roman, as they were adopted from Gaulish barbarians and were of a rough and dark fabric, in contrast to the bright and breezy Latin attire. Although Augustus prohibited their use in the Roman Forum, on account of their practicality in cold and wet weather the military used them while campaigning in hostile foreign terrain.

The inhospitable environment in which St. Michael labors is our fallen earth, where he ceaselessly fights for us in this sin-ravaged land.

He carries a globus in one hand to signify his authority. This one includes a cross on three steps, a Trinitarian allusion that reminds us of the One who gives the angel his power. The hand holding the globus is covered by his clothing—by not touching it directly, he is expressing veneration for the sacred, in much the same way we might handle something of great value lest we besmirch it. Covered hands are also a detail carried over from classical art; they call attention to the ritual and liturgical focus of the action.

Feast Day - November 8:
Synaxis of the
Archangel Michael and
all the Bodiless Powers

Kontakion, Tone IV:
Princes of God's hosts,
ministers of divine glory, *
leaders of angels and guides of
men, * pray for our welfare and
for great mercy, * O princes of
the incorporeal powers.

Saint Stephen the Archdeacon and Protomartyr

Stephen, "a man full of faith, and of the Holy Ghost" (Acts 6:5), is honored by the Church as the *protomartyr* on account of his exceptional distinction of being the first person to be martyred for Christ (Acts 22:20).

Stephen is frequently honored on iconostases because he was one of the first seven deacons to be ordained by the Church (Acts 6:5). He holds a censer in his left hand and the book of the Gospel in his right, and thus he is ready to perform his primary liturgical functions. The young man bows his head in adoration of Christ.

Behind this door, on the south wall of the sanctuary, is another door that leads to the *diaconicon*, the room where the church stores books, vessels, vestments, and other liturgical items. This room is the responsibility of the church's deacon, and thus it is natural to place near it an icon of a holy deacon.

The Diaconate

As the early Church began to grow and the number of laymen increased, it became clear to the Apostles—for they were specially responsible for the souls of men—that they needed assistance in providing for the material needs of the faithful:

> Then the twelve calling together the multitude of the disciples, said: It is not reason that we should leave the word of God, and serve tables. Wherefore, brethren, look ye out among you seven men of good reputation, full of the Holy Ghost and wisdom, whom we may appoint over this business. But we will give ourselves continually to prayer, and to the ministry of the word (Acts 6:2-4).

Stephen was named first among these. His position was humbler than the Twelve; nevertheless, being "full of grace and fortitude, [he] did great wonders and signs among the people" (Acts 6:8), manifesting the divine power bestowed upon him through his ordination.

The Catholic diaconate is the fulfillment of the role foreshadowed by the Levites in the church of the Old Covenant. The Levites were the tribe of Israel responsible for carrying the Ark of the Covenant (Dt 10) and for tending to the Tabernacle and the Temple—they functioned as assistants, musicians, singers, gatekeepers, and guardians of the treasury and of holy things (1 Par 23-26). Indeed, the title "deacon" comes from the Greek word meaning "to serve," *diakonein*.

Vesture

The protomartyr wears the liturgical vesture of the Greek-rite churches—a long, thin, white stole called an *orarion* over a purple robe known as a *sticharion*. This orarion has three golden tassels, an allusion to the Three Persons of the Trinity, and seven crosses-in-diamonds, for the Seven Holy Mysteries. The latter garment evolved from the common tunic of the early centuries AD, the chiton, which is often seen on the Apostles and holy angels.

Just peeking out from under his sticharion on his right hand is a simple brown *epimanikion*, a liturgical wrist cuff that helps to arrange the sleeves of the interior white tunic.

Incense

The burning of incense—with its captivating aromas and graceful plumes wafting heavenward—represents the prayers of the Church rising to the Most High God. It also recalls the burnt offerings of the Old Covenant, which the Scriptures

Feast Day - December 27:
Protomartyr and
Archdeacon Stephen

Troparion, Tone IV:
O apostle and first martyr
for Christ, * you fought the
good fight and exposed your
persecutors' wickedness. *
For when you were killed by
stoning at the hands of the
lawless, * you received a crown
from on high from God's right
hand, * while crying out to
Him: * "O Lord, do not hold
this sin against them."

often describe as a "sweet odour" before the throne of the Lord—His joy, of course, is not in the physical burning, but in the purity of the prayer and sacrifice offered.

The worship of the Church here on earth is a foretaste of the celestial liturgy, in which the angels ceaselessly praise the infinite God, resting "not day and night, saying: Holy, holy, holy, Lord God Almighty, who was, and who is, and who is to come" (Apoc 4:8). They are joined by the saints, whose prayers are "golden vials full of odours" (Apoc 5:8) and who proclaim to "him that sitteth on the throne, and to the Lamb, benediction, and honor, and glory, and power, for ever and ever" (Apoc 5:13).

Our prayers, which rise like smoke, are given to an angel who

> stood before the altar, having a golden censer; and there was given to him much incense, that he should offer of the prayers of all saints upon the golden altar, which is before the throne of God. And the smoke of the incense of the prayers of the saints ascended up before God from the hand of the angel (Apoc 8:3-4).

Truly, it is an honor for the deacon to bear the censer during the Divine Liturgy.

The Holy, Glorious, and All-Praised Twelve Apostles

Christ's chosen Twelve, the sure foundation upon which He built His Church, bow in awe of the great Mysteries and raise their hands in supplication for the Church still on earth.

From what we know of these men, they varied remarkably in temperament, social status, and mode of life prior to following Jesus. Together they stand as an example of God's universal call to holiness.

It should be noted that the depictions of the Apostles are not perfectly consistent, even when an attempt is made to distinguish them; they vary by time and place, and by iconographer. Some traits are more consistent than others, and some are nearly universal, even among other schools of Catholic art.

Feast Day - June 30:
Synaxis of the Holy, Glorious, and All-Praised Twelve Apostles

Troparion, Tone VIII:
O saints, your message has spread throughout the world * for receiving the Spirit in tongues of fire you torched the idol's deceit. * With the net of your words you caught those who were lost and brought them to faith. * Therefore the heavens declare your glory * and the firmament which God created adds its voice * and we with them cry out feasting your memory: * Save us all, O God, by the prayers of Your Twelve Apostles.

Daily Troparia - Thursday:
Apostles

Kontakion, Tone II:
You received Your inspired and steadfast preachers, Your chief disciples, * into the enjoyment of Your good things and into repose. * You, Who alone know the heart, accepted their labors and death * more gladly than any holocaust.

Saint James of Zebedee

Feast Day - April 30

Kontakion, Tone II:
When you heard God's voice calling out to you, * you spurned the love of your father * and fled to Christ with your kinsman, O glorious James. * With him you were favored to see the Lord's divine transfiguration.

This man is the brother of John and the child of Zebedee and Salome. Christ referred to him and his brother as *Boanerges*—the Sons of Thunder—for their energetic and manly temperaments.

The Apostle's name—taken from the patriarch Jacob—was popular in his time and place. In a quirk of linguistic progression, "Jacob" passed from Hebrew into Koine Greek, then into Latin, next into Old French, and finally found its place in English as "James."

He is the same Apostle often called James the Greater in other traditions, an epithet that distinguishes him from the other James and which alludes to his closer relationship with Christ. The Apostle is unique in that he is the only one of the Twelve whose death is recorded in Scripture (Acts 12:1-2).

James is shown as a young adult wearing the thin scruff of early manhood, also known as an *incipient beard*.

Saint Philip

Feast Day - November 14

Troparion, Tone III:
O Philip, proclaimer of God's word, * the world is adorned and Ethiopia dances for joy * for it is arrayed in beauty as with a crown. * Enlightened by you it feasts your memory. * For you taught all to believe in Christ, * finishing the course of the gospel as is right. * And so, Ethiopia boldly lifts its hands to God. * Pray to Him to grant great mercy to us.

The Gospels portray this Apostle as an unassuming, even-minded, and pious man. He exhorted the initially skeptical Nathanael to "come and see" Jesus immediately after he himself was called (Jn 1:43-46). Later, when approached by a multitude of Gentiles who wished to meet Our Lord, he came to his companion Andrew for help (Jn 12:20-22). During the Mystical Supper, he asked Jesus to show them the Father, to which request Our Lord gave His great Trinitarian and Christological reply (Jn 14).

Philip is usually depicted clean shaven, which means that he is young, probably in his late teens or early twenties. He is not to be confused with Philip the disciple and deacon, who worked miracles, preached to the Samaritans, and baptized the eunuch in the Acts of the Apostles (chapter 8).

Saint Thomas

Thomas, whose name comes from the Aramaic word for "twin," is also known as Didymus, of the same meaning in Greek.

He is most well known for doubting the reports of the Resurrection of the Lord: "Except I shall see in his hands the print of the nails, and put my finger into the place of the nails, and put my hand into his side, I will not believe" (Jn 20:25).

Yet the merciful Jesus, coming to His Apostles eight days later, said to Thomas, "Put in thy finger hither, and see my hands; and bring hither thy hand, and put it into my side; and be not faithless, but believing. Thomas answered, and said to him: My Lord, and my God" (Jn 20:27-28).

Thomas' mission took him as far as modern India, and he is considered the founder of the Church in that region. He, like Philip, is portrayed as a beardless young man.

Feast Day - October 6

Troparion, Tone II:
O disciple of Christ * and member of the apostolic council, * your lack of faith * proclaimed Christ's resurrection, * and your touch confirmed His holy passion. * O Thomas, worthy of all praise, * pray even now that He grant us peace and great mercy.

Saint Andrew the First-Called

Andrew is singular among the Twelve in that he is shown here with an *attribute*—that is, an object accompanying a person to identify him or express a concept related to him. Andrew's attribute is the X-shaped, or *saltire*, cross that he carries, a miniature of the one on which he was martyred by crucifixion. He alone of the Apostles here carries an attribute to do him special honor—he is the patron saint of Ukraine, having preached in the Dniepro River Valley, which would later develop into a part of that nation. Andrew is also considered to be the founder of the Church in Byzantion, later Constantinople, whence the Greek Rite liturgical tradition grew.

The Apostle holds the honorific "First-Called" because he was the first of the Twelve to be approached by Christ.

Andrew is depicted as an old man with a long beard; it is important to note that he appears older than Peter, his brother and fellow fisherman (Mt 4:18), whom tradition holds to be the younger sibling. His unkempt hair is an allusion to his time spent as a follower of John the Forerunner (Jn 1:35-40).

Feast Day - November 30

Kontakion, Tone II:
Let us praise God's herald, whose name is "courage,"[2] * Peter's kinsman who leads those in the Church who follow the chief apostle, * for as then to Peter so now to us he cries aloud: * "We have found the One so longed for."

[2] Some older and evidently more literal translations use the delightful "namesake of manliness" (*HT*).

Saint John the Evangelist and Theologian

Feast Day - May 8

Kontakion, Tone II:
O virgin apostle, who can recount your mighty works? *
For you pour out wonders and healings * and you pray for our souls as Theologian and friend of Christ.

The Beloved Disciple—one of the Sons of Thunder, evangelist, author of four other books of the New Testament, longest lived of the Twelve, and the only one not martyred—is shown as the young man that he was during his travels with Christ, not as the old man that he was when he wrote his Gospel and the Apocalypse.

Saint Peter, Leader of the Apostles

Feast Day - June 29:
Holy Leaders of the Apostles Peter and Paul

Troparion, Tone IV:
As the leaders of the apostles[3] * and teachers of the whole world, * intercede with the Master of all * to grant peace to the world * and to our souls great mercy.

Although Simon Bar Jona was impetuous and somewhat unreliable, Christ rewarded his great faith and love by naming him Cephas—that is, Peter, meaning Rock, the very rock upon which Christ built His church (Mt 16:18-19).

The most powerful pagan empire in history was socially conquered and spiritually converted by a relatively small group of men initially led by an unarmed, uneducated fisherman. Indeed, what else could so convincingly testify to the divine origins of this holy religion, and so sublimely manifest the power and glory of God?

The founder of the See of Rome and head of the apostolic college is given pride of place, to the right of the Eucharistic Christ on the altar during the Divine Liturgy. As is traditional, he is depicted as a man of somewhat advanced age, with white hair and a rounded beard. In this image he does not wear his traditional golden yellow.

Peter shares his feast day with the other Apostle of Rome, St. Paul.

[3] A more literal and colorful translation is, "O *first enthroned* among the apostles" (emphasis added) (*HT*).

Saint Paul, Leader of the Apostles

On the viewer's right first from the center is Paul, represented among the Twelve. Although not with Christ during His time on earth, Paul was personally chosen by the risen Savior and is considered the thirteenth Apostle. He appears here instead of Matthias, the Apostle chosen to replace Judas after the latter's betrayal (Acts 1:21-26).

Originally known as Saul of Tarsus, he was a leading Pharisee and choleric arch-persecutor of the nascent Church (Gal 1:13), yet he was personally chosen and appointed by our merciful Savior to preach His word (Acts 9).

Feast Day - June 29:
Holy Leaders of the Apostles Peter and Paul

Kontakion, Tone II:
You received Your inspired and steadfast preachers, Your chief disciples, * into the enjoyment of Your good things and into repose. * You, Who alone know the heart, accepted their labors and death * more gladly than any holocaust.

Paul is graced with a large, undulating forehead that advertises his superior wisdom and formal education; his severe grimace reveals how intently he labored for Christ. Even the tendrilous locks of his beard radiate his restless energy. As the Apostle to the Gentiles ("the nations," meaning all those who are not of Israel) and the second founder and patron of the See of Rome, Paul occupies the other position directly adjacent to Christ in the sanctuary.

Saint Jude Thaddeus, the Brother of the Lord

Author of a canonical epistle, Jude held the honor of being related to the Lord by blood (Mk 6:3), but we know little else of him. Jude was not Jesus' brother in the typical English sense of the word as a "male sibling," for Jesus had no siblings. In the Hebrew tongue, "brother" also referred to extended family, especially first cousins.

According to tradition, Jude is connected to the Image of Edessa, also called the Mandylion, a cloth with an image of Christ miraculously imprinted upon it. The Apostle received the image from Jesus and brought it to the king of Edessa, and through it Christ healed the king from an illness and worked many miracles thereafter.

Feast Day - June 19

Troparion, Tone I:
As we know you to be Christ's relative * and a steadfast martyr, * O Jude, we praise you with sacred hymns. * You trampled on error and kept the faith. * And so on this day as we feast your memory * through your prayers, O apostle, we receive release from our sins.

His name in Hebrew, Judah, was at the time quite common; to distinguish him from the infamous traitor of the same name with the temerity to betray Jesus he is called by the cognate Jude, and sometimes he is listed as Thaddeus (Mt 10:3; Mk 3:18).

In contrast to his common modern depiction, Jude is typically portrayed as an older man in both iconography and the historic schools of Western sacred art. If his hair and beard are not completely white, they are often brown, shot-through with gray or at least changed at the temples.

Saint Simon the Zealot

Feast Day - May 10

Kontakion, Tone II:
With praises let all of us call blessed * the divinely eloquent Simon. * He diligently planted the teachings of wisdom in the hearts of the godly * and stands now at the throne of glory * rejoicing with the bodiless powers and praying unceasingly for us.

Prior to his apostolic calling, Simon was known for his zeal in observing the Old Law, whence he earns his epithet (Lk 6:15). He may have been a blood relative of Christ, but the Simon mentioned in Mark 6:3 cannot be identified with certainty.

Simon is almost universally depicted as elderly—mostly bald and often, as in this image, with a rounded white beard.

Saint James of Alphaeus, the Brother of the Lord

Feast Day - October 9

Kontakion, Tone II:
With praises let us all extol James as a herald of God; * he firmly planted the doctrines of wisdom in the souls of the godly. * For he stands before the Master's throne of glory * and rejoices with all the angels * unceasingly praying for all of us.

He is also known as James the Just and is sometimes called James the Less because of the closer relationship between Jesus and the other James (of Zebedee). Despite the epithet "the Less," the son of Alphaeus was a blood relative of Christ (Mt 13:55; Gal 1:19) and wrote an epistle included among the books of the New Testament. He also had the honor of being the first bishop of Jerusalem, and he gave his name to the oldest form of the Divine Liturgy that is still in use.

His epistle is passionate, exhorting the reader to cast away "all uncleanness, and abundance of naughtiness" and "with meekness receive the ingrafted word, which is able to save your souls" (Jas 1:21). The Apostle's keen mind shines through the evocative language of the text, ripe with metaphors and similes from the natural world and which decries the sins from which we should flee so as to escape the death that they bring.

James can be identified by his brown hair and full, pointed beard.

Saint Matthew the Evangelist

Also known by the name Levi, Matthew was a former tax collector for the Roman occupation of Judea and was therefore hated by the oppressed Jews. Having been called by Christ, he readily renounced his service to the worldly king to follow the King of Kings (Lk 5:27-29).

Besides these scant facts and the honor of being an evangelist, little is known with certainty about Matthew, either from Scripture or tradition. Nevertheless, he shines forth as proof to all of us that Christ "came not to call the just, but sinners" (Mk 2:17), and his example reminds us that indeed a sinful man will often flee to God's unfailing mercy more swiftly than will those thought to be righteous.

He is depicted in the traditional manner—an older gentleman with a full head of white hair and a long white beard.

Feast Day - November 16

Kontakion, Tone IV:
Casting off the yoke of the custom house * you yoked yourself to justice; * revealed as an excellent merchant * you gained wisdom—wealth from on high. * From whence you preached the word of truth, * arousing sluggish souls by describing the hour of judgment.

Saint Bartholomew

When Philip invited Bartholomew, also called Nathanael, to meet the Savior who had come from Nazareth, Bartholomew scoffed, "Can any thing of good come from Nazareth?" (Jn 1:46). And yet, he does go to meet the Lord:

> Jesus saw Nathanael coming to him: and he saith of him: Behold an Israelite indeed, in whom there is no guile. Nathanael saith to him: Whence knowest thou me? Jesus answered, and said to him: Before that Philip called thee, when thou wast under the fig tree, I saw thee. Nathanael answered him, and said: Rabbi, thou art the Son of God, thou art the King of Israel (Jn 1:47-49).

Jesus praised Bartholomew for his lack of guile and on account of this virtue confirmed him as "an Israelite indeed," and Bartholomew immediately recognized Christ's messianic dignity. From this interchange we see that he is a serious-minded and forthright seeker of the truth. Jesus rewards this plainspoken spiritual pilgrim, promising that he "shall see the heaven opened, and the angels of God ascending and descending upon the Son of man" (Jn 1:51).

Bartholomew's facial hair is more than incipient but not nearly the full beard of later manhood.

Feast Day - June 11:
Holy Apostles
Bartholomew and Barnabas

Troparion, Tone III:
Receiving a fiery tongue in the power of the Spirit, * to all you preached the Word that has come in the flesh. * For Its sake, O Bartholomew, you were beheaded * and Barnabas endured stoning. * Together you form an adornment * for the choir of apostles. * And so we feast your memorial * and ask you to pray Christ God * to grant us forgiveness of sins.

The Four Evangelists

The men through whom the Holy Spirit wrote the four Gospels hold open their works and bow their heads in reverence to the great Mystery in the sanctuary.

Their presence on the central entrance—the Royal Doors, which symbolize, among other things, the gates of heaven—reminds us that Christ is the Way to salvation, and the evangelists lead us to Him.

In contrast to his appearance on the ceiling, John is shown in his youth, as is more typical when he is represented as an Apostle during Christ's earthly ministry. His boyish—even cherubic—visage is an unusual choice when depicting him as an evangelist.

Matthew is easily identified by his full head of white hair and long beard. These features are nearly universal in representations of him, in all schools of Christian art. The iconographer put a peculiar touch of personality to Matthew, giving him an unusually stern countenance.

Mark and Luke are not clearly distinguishable, but as Luke is more commonly depicted with a longer beard, it is safe to conclude that Mark is the upper left figure and Luke the lower.

Old Testament Figures

Righteous kings and holy messengers from the time of the church under the Old Covenant extol the goodness of God, and through *types* and other signs they proclaim the coming of Christ, in fulfillment of the Old Law and the Prophets.

A type is a special kind of symbol whereby something from the Old Covenant foreshadows or foretells something in the New Covenant. As an example, Jonas was thrown from his ship and spent three days in the belly of a whale before being released; this is a type of Christ's death and three days in the tomb before His Resurrection.

The scrolls on these icons, as with those of the evangelists on the ceiling, were not intended for close viewing, and thus the text thereon is merely representative and does not contain discernible characters.

Each bust is given a Ukrainian monogram beginning with "ПРОР," or "prophet," and then his proper name: ЕРЕМІЯ, Jeremias; МОЙСЕЙ, Moses; ІСАЯ, Isaias; СОЛОМОН, Solomon; ДАВИД, David; ІЛІЯ, Elias; ДАНИЇЛ, Daniel; and ЕЗЕКИЇЛ, Ezechiel. Although some of these individuals are not known primarily as prophets, they all did indeed prophesy. From the lower left to right:

Holy Prophet Jeremias

Feast Day - May 1

Kontakion, Tone III (*HT*):
Having cleansed thy radiant heart with the Spirit, * O glorious Jeremias, great prophet and martyr, * thou didst receive from on high the gift of prophecy * and didst cry aloud among the lands: "Behold our God! * There is none other to compare with Him, Who hath appeared, incarnate, on the earth!"

With eyes full of sorrow, Jeremias motions that he is teaching, for he speaks against the false prophets who gave easy words to the king and the people.

Jeremias foretold the defeat and subjection of Juda at the hands of the Babylonians and the vanity of waiting for help from Egypt. He preached acceptance of the punishment of God that was looming in the form of conquest, insisting that it could be an opportunity for repentance and conversion—and for this he was despised by light-minded optimists, nationalists, and kings, and he was branded as a traitor to his nation.

The prophet stood athwart the shameful acceptance of evil that characterized the later decadent kings of Juda. After the fall of Jerusalem, he was not taken into exile in Babylon, and thus he was able to continue his mission to the remnant of the Hebrew nation left in the Holy Land. Early tradition holds that he was eventually carried off to Egypt, where he was stoned to death by his own people for continually warning them against complacency amidst the forthcoming punishment of God.

Known as the "Mourning Prophet," he is the human author of two books of the Old Testament—the first, which bears his name, recounts his story, and the second, a poetic work entitled Lamentations, grieves in the most plaintive words over the loss of Jerusalem. Of the major prophets, he has the fewest instances of divine ecstasy and messianic prophecy; rather, his entire life is a type of the suffering of the coming Messiah.

He carries a scroll proclaiming, "Before I formed thee in the bowels of thy mother, I knew thee: and before thou camest forth out of the womb, I sanctified thee, and made thee a prophet unto the nations" (Jer 1:5).

Holy Prophet and God-Seer Moses

The great lawgiver's gesture indicates that he is teaching, and he holds an open scroll.

He wears a priestly turban, the robes of Near Eastern sovereigns, and a purple chlamys decorated with an *orbiculum* ornament on each shoulder. The chlamys, being a martial cape, reminds the viewer that although "Moses was a man exceeding meek above all men that dwelt upon earth" (Nm 12:3), at God's command he was courageous in battle against hostile tribes (Nm 31) and ready to apply righteous justice to disobedient schismatics (Nm 16).

His scroll should read, "May the Heavens rejoice with Him, may all the angels adore Him" (Dt 32:43).[4]

Feast Day - September 4

Troparion, Tone II (*HT*):
Thou didst ascend to the heights of the virtues, O Prophet Moses, * for which cause thou wast vouchsafed to behold the glory of God * and didst receive the grace-filled tablets of the law. * And, bearing within thyself the lineaments of grace, * thou wast the honored boast of the prophets and the great mystery of piety.

[4] This verse is from the Septuagint Greek. The verse is different in versions translated from the Hebrew. It is not in the versions elsewhere cited here.

Holy Prophet Isaias

Feast Day - May 9

Kontakion, Tone II (*HT*):
Receiving the gift of prophecy,
* O martyred Prophet Isaiah,
thou herald of God, * thou
didst explain to all the
incarnation of the Lord, *
exclaiming aloud to the ends of
the earth: * "Behold, a Virgin
shall conceive in her womb!"

The writings of Isaias contain some of the most remarkable and explicit prophecies of Christ and His Church to be found in the Old Testament, including one incident, referenced in the Divine Liturgy, that prefigures the Holy Eucharist. The prophet is given a vision of the Lord, but protests:

> I am a man of unclean lips, and I dwell in the midst of a people that hath unclean lips, and I have seen with my eyes the King the Lord of hosts. And one of the seraphims flew to me, and in his hand was a live coal, which he had taken with the tongs off the altar. And he touched my mouth, and said: Behold this hath touched thy lips, and thy iniquities shall be taken away, and thy sin shall be cleansed (Is 6:5-7).

His right hand is held up in awe and surprise at the overwhelming glory of God, and he wears a golden clavus stripe that announces his high prophetic rank.

Isaias' scroll is meant to read, "Hear, O ye heavens, and give ear, O earth, for the Lord hath spoken. I have brought up children, and exalted them: but they have despised me" (Is 1:2).

Righteous Prophet and King Solomon

King Solomon—wiser than all men that came before him (3 Kgs 3), human author of three books of the Old Testament, the richest king on earth during his time (3 Kgs 10), and builder of the first Temple in Jerusalem (3 Kgs 5-8). This towering figure ruled Israel through a time of profound peace and international prestige (3 Kgs 10:6-7).

Yet despite these singular merits, Solomon, after marrying beautiful women from pagan nations, fell into idolatry and failed in his worship of the true God. For this despicable crime, the Lord took from his son Roboam ten of the tribes of Israel and gave them to another kingdom (3 Kgs 11). The life of Solomon reminds the faithful to be careful and wise in selecting their companions and, especially, to not choose a spouse for primarily sensual reasons.

Nevertheless, the Church in her wisdom affirms that he repented before his death, and when taking his entire life into consideration she counts him among the saints. In the image, Solomon's arms are wide open as he rejoices in the goodness of the Lord. He is bedecked in regal finery, with a fiery-textured red and orange cloak. The youth ascended to the throne at about eighteen years of age, but his boyish looks are primarily intended to show that he is inferior to his father David in both age and holiness. The scroll proclaims, "Wisdom hath built herself a house, she hath hewn her out seven pillars" (Prv 9:1).

Feast Day - Sunday between December 11 and 17:
Sunday of the Holy Forefathers

Troparion, Tone II (*SB*):
Through faith, O Christ God, You justified the Patriarchs, * for through them You made a commitment to a Church with Gentiles. * These saints are glorified, because from them * descends the Virgin who gave You birth. * Through their prayers, O Christ our God, have mercy on us.

Righteous Prophet and King David

Feast Day:
Sunday of the Righteous
David, Joseph, and James -
Sunday after the Nativity

Kontakion, Tone III (*HT*):
Today godly David is filled
with joy; * Joseph and James
offer praise. * The glorious
crown of their kinship with
Christ fills them with great
joy. * They sing praises to
the One ineffably born on
earth, * and they cry out: "O
Compassionate One, save those
who honor You!"

The second king of Israel and the glorious founder of the dynasty of the kings of Juda, David was a man after God's own heart (Acts 13:22), filled with humble piety and righteous deeds. He was so pleasing to the Lord that He promised David that there "shall not fail a man of thy race upon the throne of Israel" (3 Kgs 9:5). This vow was fulfilled not only in the temporal rule of the Jewish people but also in David's greatest descendent, namely, Our Lord Jesus Christ, the eternal King of the New Israel.

David is also honored as the primary author of the Psalms, the songbook of the Church.

Although David was not without his faults (2 Kgs 11-12), Holy Writ exclaims that of the more than twenty kings of Juda, "all committed sin" except for David and two others (Ecclus 49:1-6). Those who are disillusioned by the many failures of Church leadership, both now and in the past, would do well to remember God's tender mercy and steadfast support for His people as they endured such a sorry group of leaders as the kings of Juda—not to mention the blatantly idolatrous kings of northern Israel. In light of this, the comparatively minor flaws of the New Covenant's human authorities are no excuse for the believing Christian to not embrace the Catholic Church.

David is dressed in a fashion similar to that of his son Solomon, but even more sumptuous, and he is adorned by an elegant and tightly curled classical hairstyle. The psalmist holds up his hand in wonder, glorifying the power of the Lord.

His scroll should say, "How great are thy works, O Lord? thou hast made all things in wisdom: the earth is filled with thy riches" (Ps 103:24).

Holy and Glorious Prophet Elias

This most glorious prophet of the Old Testament worked many mighty deeds, including raising a boy from the dead (3 Kgs 17:17-24). His mission was directed primarily against the evil King Achab of Israel and his Sidonian wife Jezabel, a priestess of the false gods of her native people (3 Kgs 16ff.). In response to the king's continuing schism and the queen's cruel murder of God's people, Elias challenged 450 false prophets to show that their alleged gods could answer their prayers; when they failed miserably, Elias called down fire from heaven to show that the Lord of Israel is the true God, and he had the 450 killed (3 Kgs 18).

Elias left this life while he was walking with his follower Eliseus: as they were "talking together, behold a fiery chariot, and fiery horses parted them both asunder: and Elias went up by a whirlwind into heaven" (4 Kgs 2:11). He and the patriarch Henoch (Gn 5:23-24) are the only two men in Scripture who are described as ascending directly to heaven. Elias was prophesied to return "before the coming of the great and dreadful day of the Lord" (Mal 4:5); this prophecy was fulfilled in the person of John the Forerunner (Mt 17:10-13). According to an ancient and common interpretation, Elias and Henoch are the "two witnesses" (Apoc 11:3) whom Christ will send to prophesy before the end of the world.

The prophet makes a gesture of blessing, likely directed to Eliseus, and he holds a closed scroll.

Elias wears a rough animal skin cloak, an *addereth*, that calls to mind blood sacrifice and atonement. It is also a symbol of his prophetic office and was passed on to his successor Eliseus (4 Kgs 2). Around his neck he wears a prayer shawl known as a *tallit*.

Feast Day - July 20

Troparion, Tone IV:
The glorious Elias—angelic in body, pillar of prophets, * second herald of Christ * by sending grace upon Eliseus from on high, * dispels disease, cleanses lepers, * and overflows with healing for those who honor him.

Holy Prophet Daniel

Feast Day - December 17:
Holy Prophet Daniel
and Three Holy Youths

Kontakion, Tone III (*HT*):
Enlightened by the Spirit, *
thy pure heart became the
receptacle of most splendid
prophecy: * for thou beheldest
far-off things as though they
were present, * and, cast into
the pit, didst tame the lions. *
Wherefore, we honor thee, O
blessed and glorious Prophet
Daniel.

This young man was among the unfortunate Judeans to be carried off to Babylon by the conqueror Nebuchadnezzar. On account of his grace and exceptional wisdom, he quickly found favor in the court of his new king (Dn 1:1-6). Though he was forced to live amidst the idolatrous Chaldeans, Daniel retained his righteousness and exhibited heroic perseverance in the ways of God (Dn 1:6-20).

The youth became a court favorite, interpreting dreams and divine signs for the kings of Babylon (Dn 2,4,5). He defended the wrongly accused against corrupt civil authorities (Dn 13); demonstrated the folly of idol worship and the power of the true God (Dn 3,5,14); and conversed with angels about future events, especially the coming of Christ and the desolation of Jerusalem. Through types and symbols he also prophesied the eventual reign of Antichrist (Dn 7-12).

Daniel carries a closed scroll in one hand. The other hand is raised to show surprise and thanksgiving in regards to God's generosity in saving him from ravenous lions, to which he was twice thrown (Dn 6,14). The prophet is dressed in a Persian style to indicate that he lived during the Babylonian Captivity. His headwear—a turban from which a small, red, cone-shaped hat rises—was common for Jews of the Middle Ages in the Eastern Roman Empire, and thus it identifies him as Jewish.

Holy Prophet Ezechiel

This man of the priestly line prophesied before and during the Babylonian Captivity, at roughly the same time as Jeremias, but unlike the latter he was one of the Hebrews to be carried off into exile.

Ezechiel's writings are filled with swirling prophetic and mystical visions, including symbolic depictions of the throne of the Lord and the court of His angels in heaven (Ez 1ff.).

Through Ezechiel, God paints for the inhabitants of Jerusalem pictures of their decadence, comparing them to a rusty pot that will break in a fire (Ez 24:6-11) and to dead vines to be burned (Ez 15). The Lord, by metaphor, describes Juda as an ungrateful wife who has prostituted herself to others by indulging in idolatry and the other heinous crimes of her pagan neighbors (Ez 16:1-34ff.). God foretells to Ezechiel that his wife—"the desire of [his] eyes" (Ez 24:16)—will die, but He does not allow the prophet to mourn; instead, he becomes a living lesson to the Hebrew captives, warning them against excessive grief amidst the loss of temporal blessings, for God should be their deepest source of joy (Ez 24:15-25).

But in the end, the Lord consoles His people, assuring them of the reunification of the temporal Israel and, ultimately, of the coming of the Messiah, who will remake the people of God as the New Israel. Thus, Ezechiel's scroll should proclaim, "Thus saith the Lord God: Behold I myself will seek my sheep, and will visit them" (Ez 34:11).

Feast Day - July 21

Kontakion, Tone IV (*HT*):
Thou hast been shown to be a prophet of God, * O wondrous Ezekiel, * and hast proclaimed unto all the incarnation of the Lord, * the Lamb and Creator, * the Son of God Who hath revealed Himself forever.

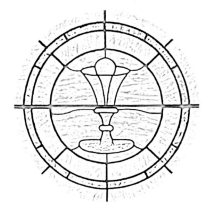

Chapter 3:
Side Shrines

For by so much more frequently as [the holy images] are seen in artistic representation, by so much more readily are men lifted up to the memory of their prototypes, and to a longing after them; and to these should be given due salutation and honorable reverence... incense and lights may be offered according to ancient pious custom.

-Decree of the Second Council of Nicaea
AD 787

Feast Day:
Protection of Our Most Holy Lady, the Mother of God and Ever-Virgin Mary - October 1

Troparion, Tone IV:
Today we believers radiantly celebrate, * flooded in light by your coming to us, O Mother of God; * beholding your pure image, * we say with contrition: * shelter us with your precious protection[5] * and deliver us from every evil, * entreating your Son, Christ our God, to save our souls.

[5] A more literal translation uses the tangible and appealing, "extend your holy mantle over us" (*SB*).

Protection of the Mother of God

Our blessed and glorious Lady stands in supplication before Our Lord, praying for us and placing her mantle of protection over us.

This icon and its related devotion originated in AD 911 in Constantinople as it was besieged by Saracen armies. A portion of the populace had fled to the Church of the Mother of God at Blachernae, including St. Andrew the Fool-for-Christ, a Slav by birth, and his disciple St. Epiphanius. While praying for deliverance from the enemy, Andrew saw the Mother of God, flanked by saints and angels, descend into the church. Our Lady asked her Son to accept the prayers of those present; she then prayed for them herself and spread her white veil over the people to protect them.

This miracle was witnessed by both saints and a large group of others; indeed, Constantinople not only survived the attack but endured another 542 years of nearly constant foreign aggression.

An icon was commissioned to commemorate the event, and the image supposedly records the heavenly vision just as Andrew saw it. The original icon was venerated in the church where the incident occurred, and its popularity spread. Our icon descends from this ancient work.

Mary continues to offer her prayers for us—she always has and always will. Should we humbly flee to her protection, she will always be our loving guardian.

In other versions of this icon, the Constantinople skyline or the assembled crowd are visible underneath the Virgin's veil. And this image contains an unusual feature—the colors of the Mother of God's clothes, with a blue maphorion over a red chiton, are reversed from the typical usage.

Saint Nicholas the Wonderworker

Nicholas—bishop of Myra in Lycia, worker of miracles, lover of the poor, and patron of this church—holds the Gospels with his reverently covered left hand and raises his right hand in blessing.

Perhaps the most beloved saint in all of Christendom, Nicholas is revered for his enormous charity—he gave his inherited wealth away anonymously to those in need, most famously to three poor young ladies in need of dowries. God worked countless miracles through his intercession, from healing the sick and preventing famines to extinguishing fires and repelling foreign armies.

Scant facts are known about the wonderworker's life, but it is fairly certain that he was imprisoned during the persecution of the Church by the Emperor Diocletian. He protected his see from the Arian heresy, and he may also have attended the First Council of Nicaea in AD 325.

The beloved saint's large forehead expresses his exceptional wisdom. He wears a stole decorated with crosses, an *omophorion*, over a purple vestment known as a *sakkos*. Both signify his office of bishop. Near his knees and below is visible another type of stole, a brown *epitrachelion*, which is worn by both priests and bishops.

Feast Day:
Our Father among the Saints, Nicholas, Archbishop and Wonderworker of Myra in Lycia - December 6

Also,

Daily Troparia:
Thursday - St. Nicholas

Troparion, Tone IV:
The truth of your deeds made you for your flock a rule of faith * and an image of meekness, * a teacher of continence. * And so you gained the heights through humility, * riches through poverty, * father and bishop Nicholas. * Intercede with Christ our God * for the salvation of our souls.

Saints Vladimir and Olha

Vladimir the Great, grand prince of Kyiv and converter of the Rus', grasps a cross-headed scepter representing his temporal authority. His grandmother, the Holy Equal-to-the-Apostles Olha, holds up the pre-renovation Cathedral of St. Sophia in Kyiv.

The Saints in Glory

Although in the image she appears to be the younger, Olha is Vladimir's grandmother, and so an idealized form is used. The viewer sees not a realistic family portrait but rather a representation of what the pair may look like glorified in heaven.

Olha was baptized later in life, in Constantinople in AD 959. After the death of her husband, she ruled as a regent for her son Sviatoslav. She tried to bring about the conversion of her lands, but she enjoyed limited success because her son and much of the ruling class remained pagan and thwarted her efforts.

Yet, Olha prepared the ground for a later harvest after her death.

According to St. Nestor the Chronicler, in the late tenth century Vladimir set out to find a religion for his largely pagan populace. Emissaries were dispatched to explore the faiths of the surrounding civilizations. Islam was rejected for its gloom and prohibition of alcohol, and Judaism's loss of Jerusalem was perceived as a sign of divine disfavor. Regarding Christianity, his envoys were not impressed by the plainness of Germanic Latin Catholicism. However, when they beheld the full flowering beauty of the Greek Divine Liturgy in Constantinople, they "no longer knew whether [they] were in heaven or on earth, but only knew that God dwells there among men." In AD 988, Vladimir summarily converted, negotiated a military alliance with the Eastern Roman Empire, married into the imperial family, and encouraged the mass baptism of his populace.

Regalia

Both rulers wear crowns typical of the emperors in Constantinople and of other cultures watered by it. Vladimir's crown is adorned with Eastern Roman–style dangling *pendilia*, only one of which is visible.

Draped around Olha's head, neck, and shoulders is a popular medieval women's garment called a *wimple*.

On Vladimir's shoulder is a circular patch of embroidery called an orbiculum. His bears a cross, though orbiculi were used for many types of decorations or to show the rank of the wearer. At a time when both clothing and embroidered decorations were expensive, the orbiculi could be removed from a worn-out garment and fastened to a new one. Also, the orbiculi could be changed according to the wearer's circumstances such that it was not necessary to own multiple sets of fine clothing.

Feast Day:
Holy Equal-to-the-Apostles Great Prince Vladimir, in Holy Baptism called Basil, enlightener of Rus' - July 15

Troparion, Tone IV:
You resembled the merchant who sought the pearl of great price, * O Vladimir, glorious in might: * seated on the throne of Kiev, the divinely saved mother of the cities of Rus', * as a seeker you sent envoys to the Imperial City to know the orthodox faith, * and found Christ the pearl, who chose you as another Paul, * and removed your blindness both spiritual and bodily in the holy font. * Therefore we, your people, feast your falling asleep. * Pray the leaders of Rus' be saved with those entrusted to them.

Feast Day:
Blessed Equal-to-the-Apostles Olha, in Holy Baptism called Helen, Princess of Kyiv - July 11

Troparion, Tone IV:
On the wings of the knowledge of God * you lifted your mind, O glorious Olha * and soared beyond the visible * attaining to God, the Creator of all. * You found Him and in baptism received the new life * abiding forever in incorruption * and enjoying the fruits of the life-giving Tree.

Chi-Rho

This monogram for Christ, a *christogram* as it is called, is flanked by an alpha and omega in the less common lowercase script: ⍺ ⍵. It adorns the area to the viewer's lower left of Vladimir and Olha.

Chi and rho, X and P, the first two letters of "Christ" in Greek, are imposed upon each other to make the symbol.

Monograms

Combining two or more letters into one symbol has long been a popular way to make a monogram; even today this method is employed by royalty, corporations, and sports teams. During Late Antiquity, this kind of monogram was used as a signature by powerful men, artists, craftsmen, and others in every level of society.

It follows naturally that early Christians would display a christogram to identify themselves as followers of Our Lord, and this symbol continues to be popular among the faithful. The IHS seen in the art of the Latin Church is another example of a christogram, and there are many others as well.

Appearance to Constantine the Great

The chi-rho has been recognized as a Christian symbol from the earliest times. In AD 312, before the great Battle of the Milvian Bridge against the usurping challenger Maxentius, the Equal-to-the-Apostles Emperor Constantine the Great, not yet converted from paganism, saw this figure in the sky, along with the Greek words Ἐν τούτῳ νίκα, *En touto nika* —"In this (sign), (you will) conquer." Constantine applied the symbol to the shields of his soldiers and decisively won the battle, routing the pretender.

Later, during his ultimately successful conflict with his pagan co-emperor Licinius, he applied the chi-rho to his *labarum*, a type of Roman battle flag. After this victory, Constantine was the sole legitimate emperor, and he reigned over all the lands of Rome for another twelve years. During this time—thanks to his victories and his legalization and patronage of Christianity—his favored symbol, the chi-rho, became immensely popular.

**Holy Equal-to-the-Apostles
Emperor Constantine and
Helena, His Mother** - May 21

Troparion, Tone VIII:
After seeing the image of
Your cross in the heavens,
O Lord, * and receiving like
Paul the summons that was
not from men, * Your apostle
among kings entrusted into
Your hands the imperial city. *
Always save it in peace by the
prayers of the Mother of God,
* only Lover of mankind.

Cathedral of Saint Sophia

Saint Sophia is not a person but a personification of "Holy Wisdom," from the Greek meaning exactly that, Ἁγία Σοφία, *Hagia Sophia*. Construction was completed on May 11, 1018, by Yaroslav I the Wise, son of and successor to St. Vladimir. It still contains the tomb of its royal builder.

The cathedral appears as it was while used by Catholics following the Union of Brest in 1595, when a large portion of Ukraine re-entered the Catholic communion and the modern Ukrainian Greek Catholic Church was born. This arrangement was short-lived, though, for in 1633 the building was claimed by the Orthodox, who remodeled it with green, multi-tiered Ukrainian Baroque–style domes.

This expressive icon shows St. Sophia as it was during its brief Catholic ownership four centuries ago and presents it in the loving embrace of one of Ukraine's foundational saints.

House of Wisdom

The Book of Proverbs speaks eloquently of Wisdom and reveals the beauty of dedicating a church with this name, as it speaks, spiritually, that:

> Wisdom hath built herself a house, she hath hewn her out seven pillars. She hath slain her victims, mingled her wine, and set forth her table. She hath sent her maids to invite to the tower, and to the walls of the city: Whosoever is a little one, let him come to me. And to the unwise she said: Come, eat my bread, and drink the wine which I have mingled for you. Forsake childishness, and live, and walk by the ways of prudence (Prv 9:1-6).

Adding to the popularity of the name St. Sophia in the Greek rites is the great mother church of Constantinople, that magnificent structure built by Emperor Justinian the Great—St. Sophia in Constantinople. So beautiful was the cathedral that upon its completion, Justinian compared it to the glory of the first Temple of Jerusalem and declared, "O Solomon, I have surpassed thee!"

Feast Day:
Dedication of the Cathedral
of St. Sophia in Kyiv - May 11

Psalm 146:1-5
Praise ye the Lord, because
psalm is good: to our God be
joyful and comely praise. * The
Lord buildeth up Jerusalem:
he will gather together the
dispersed of Israel. * Who
healeth the broken of heart,
and bindeth up their bruises.
* Who telleth the number of
the stars: and calleth them
all by their names. * Great
is our Lord, and great is his
power: and of his wisdom
there is no number.

Troparion, Tone IV:
You appeared as a radiant light,
* O priest-martyr Josaphat. *
Like the Good Shepherd, you
lay down your life for your
sheep; * killed by enemies who
loved division,[6] you entered the
holy of holies to dwell with the
bodiless powers. * Therefore
we pray you, long-suffering
saint: * beg Christ, the Prince
of Shepherds, * to number us
among the sheep at his right
hand and to save our souls.

[6] An older and more plainspoken
translation is, "You were slain
by the lovers of heresy" (*SB*).

Saint Josaphat Kuntsevych of Polotsk

The bishop and saint holds the palm of martyrdom, the axe with which he was killed, and a *crozier*, a type of staff carried by bishops as a symbol of their office.

The saint dedicated his life to serving the poor, reforming the lax clergy, and working for the reunion of the Catholic and Orthodox churches. He wrote several religious texts, including a catechism for the priests under his care. Josaphat's deep kindness, dedication to preaching and hearing confessions, and severe personal mortifications gained many converts to Catholicism, including Russian Orthodox Patriarch Ignatius of Moscow and a member of the Eastern Roman imperial family, Emmanuel Cantacuzenus.

Martyrdom

Josaphat lived at a time when the reunion of the Ukrainian church with Rome was still fresh. Individual and community attachment to Catholic or Orthodox communion was often in flux, and the secular powers maneuvered in religious affairs for political gain; emotions ran high.

The saint was a voice for calm and compassion amidst the strife, yet he never sacrificed his principles for a false peace. Unfortunately, he faced opposition from almost every corner. The Orthodox were hostile to reunion, and they induced many Ukrainian Catholics to separate once again from Rome. And some among the Latin Church were of a conformist mindset that would uniformly impose the Roman Rite on all Catholics, and thus they objected to Josaphat's rightful insistence that his people retain their Greek Rite heritage.

Eventually, the hostility reached a fevered pitch. Separatists boldly set up rival bishops in many areas that had already reunited with Rome. When the king of Poland, who controlled the territory at that time, declared Josaphat to be the rightful archbishop of Polotsk, riots broke out.

The opposition attempted to incite Josaphat to violence, in an attempt to get rid of him. One Orthodox priest in particular, Elias, went to Josaphat's lodgings and spent the day verbally abusing and threatening him, his friends, and Rome. The saint's distressed servants pleaded with him for permission to do something, but he would only allow them to lock Elias away should he again try to foment trouble. The priest returned the next day to take up his tirades again, so the beleaguered servants held him in a room of the house. When Josaphat returned and assessed the situation, he released the priest.

Elias was unharmed, but the separatists had the excuse they needed. Signal bells were rung around the city of Vitebsk, and a violent mob gathered at Josaphat's residence and began to assault his friends and servants. Seeing the violence, the saint pleaded with them to leave his loved ones alone and take up their grievances directly with him. He was promptly beaten with a stick and hacked up with an axe, and the *coup de grâce* was delivered by a bullet to the head. His lifeless body, along with that of a dog that tried to defend him, was then cast into a river.

The violence backfired, for as a result of his martyrdom public opinion swung back to the cause of Catholic unity. Many repented, and even the rival archbishop of Polotsk, Meletius Smotritsky, was reconciled with Rome.

In 1867, Josaphat became the first Eastern Catholic to be formally declared a saint by the pope since Rome established the modern canonization process during the twelfth and thirteenth centuries. He was also the first Ukrainian Catholic saint added to the Ukrainian Catholic Church's calendar since its reunion with Rome in 1597.

Vestments and Attributes

Josaphat wears a white omophorion over a purple bishop's cape, a *mantiya*; a bishop's *pectoral cross* hangs from his neck. On the crown of his head he wears a purple *phiro*, a type of priestly skullcap.

His crozier is topped with a globus cruciger, and two snakes are wound around it. The snakes show that the bishop's work is to heal—this symbolism is derived primarily from Numbers 21:4-9, in which Moses, at God's command, uses a brazen serpent on a pole to heal the Hebrews who were suffering from snakebites. The ancient world would also have been familiar with the *Rod of Asclepius*, a branch with a snake wound about it, which was associated with health and medicine.

The saint carries the palm of martyrdom: an ancient symbol of victory, the palm is well known among Christians because it was used by the adoring crowd during Christ's entrance into Jerusalem (Jn 12:13). The martyr's palm is common in Western sacred art, but it is unusual in iconography.

Kontakion, Tone IV:
By Your own choice, O Christ
our God, * You were lifted on
the cross. * Grant Your mercies
to Your new community that
bears Your Name. * By Your
power gladden the faithful
people * and grant them
victory against enemies. *
May they have the help of
Your instrument of peace, the
invincible sign of victory.[7]

Greek Cross

This cross with two bars of equal length set in the middle of each other, called a *Greek cross*, is emblazoned with ICXC NIKA—"Jesus Christ Conquers." It decorates the space to the viewer's right of St. Josaphat. This message, another type of christogram, proclaims that the cross is both the sign of our blessed Savior's glorious triumph and the weapon by which He accomplished it.

Although Christ is certainly a conqueror in the human and physical realm, as were St. Constantine and many other great men, here we profess Christ's vastly more important victory over the world and the ancient Enemy, and especially over sin and death (Lk 18:33; Jn 8:52; 2 Tm 1:10).

This is a triumph in which Our Lord wishes us to participate; we must proclaim it to the world, so that all of mankind may also join Him. ICXC NIKA therefore reminds us that Christ is the eternal Conqueror and also calls us to rally ourselves and others to His cause.

This message is so important that the symbol seen here is stamped onto every *prosphoron*, that is, the loaf of bread to be consecrated during the Divine Liturgy.

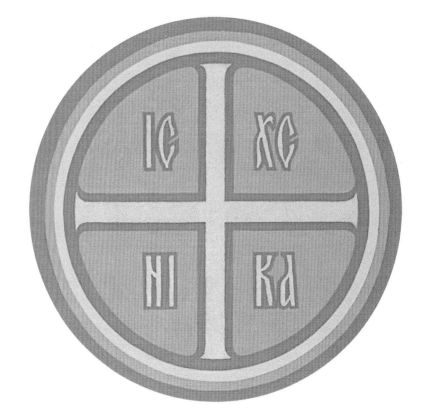

[7] Older translations, apparently more literal, use the more evocative, "May she have as Thy help the invincible trophy, the weapon of peace" (*HT*), or a similar wording (*SB*).

Cathedral of Saint George

At the time this icon was installed in the mid twentieth century, this cathedral in Lviv was the seat of the Ukrainian Greek Catholic Church, as it was from the nineteenth century until 2005.

It is likely that this image was intentionally situated near St. Josaphat because both were deeply involved in controversies of reunion. In July of 1700, the Act of Unification of the Lviv Archeparchy to Rome was proclaimed here.

During March of 1946, the Synod of Lviv—orchestrated by the Soviets—was held in St. George's; this Synod forced the members of the hierarchy who were not already imprisoned to renounce Catholic unity and join the Russian Orthodox Church.

The communists took their foot off the throat of the UGCC in 1989, and the cathedral was returned to its rightful owners on August 14, 1990.

In August of 2005, the patriarchate was moved to Kyiv, and since that time St. George's has been the seat of the archbishop of Lviv.

The current Ukrainian Baroque structure, the third version of the cathedral, dates from the middle of the eighteenth century; the first was erected in the thirteenth century.

Many heroes of the UGCC are buried here, including Major Metropolitan Josyf Slipyj, Metropolitans Andrei Sheptytsky and Volodymyr Sterniuk, and Cardinals Myroslav Ivan Lubachivsky and Sylvester Sembratovych.

Feast Day:
Dedication of the Cathedral of St. George in Lviv - November 27

Psalm 11:2-5
Save me, O Lord, for there is now no saint: truths are decayed from among the children of men. * They have spoken vain things every one to his neighbor: with deceitful lips, and with a double heart have they spoken. * May the Lord destroy all deceitful lips, and the tongue that speaketh proud things. * Who have said: We will magnify our tongue; our lips are our own; who is Lord over us?

Chapter 4:
Vault Feasts and Scenes

It is our duty to present to God, like sacrifices, all the festivals and hymnal celebrations; and first of all, (the feast of) the Annunciation to the holy Mother of God, to wit, the salutation made to her by the angel, "Hail, full of grace!"

-St. Gregory the Wonderworker
Four Homilies, AD 262

Twelve Great Feasts

Also called the *Dodecaorton*, these are the days on which the Church celebrates twelve principal events in salvation history. In times past, the faithful were expected to keep all of them as holy days and attend Divine Liturgy, and the dates were often civil holidays as well.

The Twelve Great Feasts are:

- Nativity of the Mother of God
- Exaltation of the Cross
- Presentation of the Mother of God
- Nativity of Our Lord
- Theophany
- Presentation of Our Lord, its icon entitled *Holy Meeting of Our Lord*
- Annunciation to the Mother of God
- Palm/Willow Sunday, its icon entitled *Entrance into Jerusalem*
- Ascension of Our Lord
- Descent of the Holy Spirit
- Transfiguration
- Dormition of the Mother of God

Notably absent from the list is Pascha, because it always falls on a Sunday. But Christ's glorious conquest of death is most explicitly celebrated by the *Anastasis* icon which is considered in the next chapter, though *Descent of Our Lord from the Cross* and *Myrrh-Bearing Women* also testify to the Paschal Mystery.

The feasts are well represented in St. Nicholas Church, but they are not arranged together; instead, they are mingled with other sacred events of similar themes.

The Vault

The eight icons on the vault are divided into the scenes related to the life of Our Lady on the left and to the life of Our Lord on the right.

Several festal icons that do not appear here—those for the Nativity of Our Lord, the Theophany, the Entrance into Jerusalem, and the Transfiguration—were already present in the church at the time that the vault icons were chosen. The images for the Ascension and the Exaltation of the Cross are not installed elsewhere, but they could not be placed here because they are strongly vertical in shape.

Two scenes appear on the vault that are not Great Feasts: *Descent of Our Lord from the Cross* and *Myrrh-Bearing Women*.

Mary Side

Through the course of the liturgical year, the Church represents to the faithful the drama of salvation history, and thus the cycle of each year takes the faithful on a spiritual journey through the entirety of God's work among men. The repetition of the fixed and movable feasts, the calendar of saints, and the progression of liturgical seasons join with the splendor of the Divine Liturgy and the ineffable Mystery of the Eucharist to continually bestow upon the pious Catholic a supernaturally timeless perspective of history and, even more importantly, a foretaste of the love, knowledge, and ecstacy that awaits us in eternity.

The liturgical year begins on September 1, and the Church honors the Mother of God by beginning the year with one of her feasts, that of her birth, on September 8, and closing it out with the feast of her holy Dormition on August 15.

The Church thus impresses upon her children the necessity of Mary in our salvation and encourages us to be devoted to her. Year after year, we begin and end our spiritual quest with the glorious Queen of Heaven—She Who Shows the Way—whose mysteries and virtues will be praised and loved by the blessed through ages and ages.

Christ Side

The first three icons on this side all relate directly to Our Lord's Passion and Resurrection—from the prophecy of Simeon, through the mournful completion of His labors on Golgotha, to the first of His followers to witness His victory.

The final icon, *Descent of the Holy Spirit*, marks the birth of the Church and the beginning of that astounding evangelization which would carry the glories of Christ's Resurrection to the ends of the earth.

Nativity of the Mother of God

The Holy and Righteous Saints Joachim and Anna were married for fifty years, suffering the "reproach of childlessness," before God finally granted their prayers for a child.

Anna reclines after giving birth to the Mother of God. One handmaiden fans her; another brings water for refreshment; and a third presents her with eggs, a symbol of fertility. To the lower right, a midwife washes the swaddled newborn Mary as she is held by a servant girl.

In accordance with rabbinical law, Joachim sits at a distance; the blue curtain indicates that he is actually in another room and not present at the birth. He stretches out his arm in amazement, for the gracious God has allowed them to be parents so late in life.

The Eighth Day

Catholics worship on the "Eighth Day" of the week—that is, Sunday, the day on which Christ rose from the dead (Mk 16:2,9). This Eighth Day also leads to the new era of salvation history inaugurated by Christ, for it is the first day of the "new week" in the relationship between God and man. As a reflection of this great truth, the Nativity of the Mother of God, which is considered the beginning of the immediate preparation for Christ's mission, is celebrated on the eighth day of the liturgical year, September 8.

Joachim and Anna

The birth of a child to an elderly infertile couple is also a foreshadowing of the even more miraculous birth by a virgin. The couple's old age is seen in their sunken cheeks and in Joachim's silvery hair. The gift of eggs further highlights the miraculous gift of fertility given by God.

Anna wears the blue cowl of marriage around her hair, as we typically see on the Mother of God as an adult. She is depicted in orange and green, the opposing colors of blue and red, so that the viewer immediately understands that the image portrays Anna rather than Mary.

Joachim's lack of involvement in the main action resembles portrayals of Joseph in icons of the Nativity of Our Lord, and it thus serves as a visual cue linking the two events.

The fan is modeled after the *ripidion*, the sacred fan historically used during the consecration in the Divine Liturgy, and thus it highlights the sanctity of Anna. As of this writing, a ripidion bearing an icon of St. Nicholas rests in the left aisle of the nave of the church.

Mary and Her Attendants

Another visual cue tying this scene to Christ's birth is the striking visual similarity between the portrayal of the newborns with their basins and attendants. In both Nativity icons, the washbasin is reminiscent of a baptismal font. About the outside are decorative shells, an early symbol for baptism employed frequently in Late Antique Christian art.

The child Virgin here is depicted as a small adult, as is typical of Christ as a youth. Although Our Lady does not hold the fullness of Wisdom that Our Lord does, she is without the stain of sin, and thus it may be said that she is already fully mature in moral perfection.

Most of the females have red footwear, which in this icon is incidental and not indicative of royal status as it is when used for Our Lady. Indeed, the servant girl attending to Mary wears a practical headscarf that identifies her as a member of the servant class. Anna's attendants, however, are garbed in the style of courtly citizens of Constantinople.

The midwife is shown with an uncovered head, having neither a fillet nor a cowl to indicate her marital status; this is unusual in iconographic depictions of women from biblical times.

The Apocrypha

The iconography for the Nativity of the Mother of God draws most of its imagery from a source known as the *Protoevangelion of James*, which outlines many events that supposedly occurred in the lives of Christ and Mary but are not recorded in the New Testament.

There is much early literature of this type, and it is collectively called the *apocrypha*, from the Greek for "hidden." If a work is labeled apocryphal, this merely means that it is not considered divinely inspired and therefore is not included in the biblical canon. The work is thus considered fully human, but the term implies no further judgment regarding its veracity.

Several of these texts are simply a patchwork of legends, and some were written with hostile intentions by the enemies of the Church. But many of them contain actual history and verbal traditions that were eventually written down to satisfy the natural curiosity of the faithful regarding many details of the Holy Family's life that are not discussed in Scripture. Although perhaps not written according to the same standards as modern historical scholarship, the apocrypha are not necessarily less true than other oral or textual traditions found among such venerable figures as Plato, Plutarch, or Eusebius. Each work of the apocrypha must be judged on its own merits.

In addition, Catholics should recall that some other Christians mistakenly label seven canonical books of the Bible as "apocrypha": Tobit, Judith, Wisdom, Ecclesiasticus, Baruch, and 1 and 2 Machabees, along with portions of Esther and Daniel.

Feast Day - September 8:
The Nativity of Our Most Holy Lady, the Mother of God and Ever-Virgin Mary

Kontakion, Tone IV:
By your birth, O Immaculate One, * Joachim and Anna were freed from the reproach of childlessness, * and Adam and Eve from the corruption of death. * And your people, redeemed from the guilt of their sins, celebrate as they cry out to you: * "The barren one gives birth to the Mother of God and nourisher of our life."

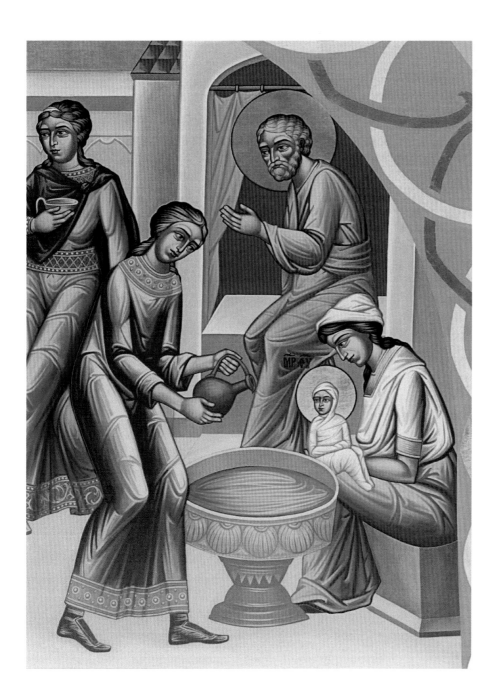

Presentation of the Mother of God in the Temple

Joachim and Anna, when praying for a child, had promised to consecrate any offspring to the service of God. Joachim wished to take Mary immediately to the Temple, but Anna asked that they wait until she was three years of age so that she would have less need of her human parents.

The image depicts this profound moment, when the aged saints take their daughter to the priest Zacharias for a blessing; they bow and motion that they are offering Mary to serve the Lord through prayer in His Temple.

Accompanying them are four chaste maidens of Israel carrying lights; these women were invited by Joachim in the hope that they would encourage Mary to be captivated by the Temple and not desire to turn back to her parents.

Foreshadowing

The Presentation foreshadows the Holy Meeting of Our Lord, when Mary and Joseph bring Christ to the Temple. In this we see a part of the complex web of prefigurements of Christ's life that occurred in the lives of His near family members and immediate ancestors. The iconography for the Presentation also relies on the *Protoevangelion of James.*

Mary and Zacharias

Although the *Protoevangelion* does not mention the name of the priest who consecrates Mary, Zacharias eventually figures into the text. Zacharias would later take part in the second of the three miraculous pregnancies that directly preceded the

New Covenant, when his aged wife Elizabeth conceived John the Forerunner (Lk 1). It is therefore common to identify him as the priest in this icon.

Mary's hands are covered, emphasizing the ritual aspect of the scene. Her parents and the nearer two handmaidens bow to her and Zacharias, both of whom stand on a raised platform to indicate their greater holiness; Zacharias, in turn, bows to Our Lady as he consecrates her.

Typically, an unmarried woman—as Mary clearly would be at this age—would wear a fillet tie in her hair, but the blue kekryphalos coif of a wedded lady is universally connected to Mary and thus the iconographer decided to depict her that way.

Zacharias wears the small turban and hat that identify him as living under the Old Covenant. Priests under the Old Law did wear turbans, although this one is smaller and not necessarily intended to represent clerical garb. He wears a simplified version of the sky-blue priestly robe (Ex 28:31-32). Zacharias also has a finely embroidered chlamys cape, pinned at the neck. The chlamys was not part of Judean liturgical clothing but rather descends from imperial fashions of Constantinople; the ornate beauty of his clothing corresponds to his spiritual status.

The Two Arks

Behind the priest is a simplified representation of the Temple veil, behind which resides the Ark of the Covenant. The Ark is a type of Our Lady, who is the Ark of the New Covenant because she carried Our Lord, the source of the New Law, as the prior vessel carried the Stone Tablets, the symbolic source of the Old Law. Mary is also most pure, as was the gold of the Ark (Ex 25:11); she was untouched by man (2 Kgs 6:7); and she is one before whom prophets and kings rejoice (Lk 1:41; 2 Kgs 6:16)—among numerous other comparisons.

Feast Day - November 21:
The Entry of the Most Holy Mother of God into the Temple

Kontakion, Tone IV:
The Savior's pure temple, * the precious bridal chamber and Virgin, * the sacred treasury of the glory of God, * is brought today into the house of the Lord; * and with her she brings the grace * of the divine Spirit. * God's angels sing in praise of her. * She is indeed the heavenly dwelling place.[8]

[8] Older versions use the more scripturally evocative translation, "She is the heavenly tabernacle!" (*HT*; cf. *SB*).

Annunciation to the Mother of God

One of heaven's great ambassadors, the Archangel Gabriel, arrives with wings alight and feet in urgent motion: "The angel being come in, said unto her: Hail, full of grace, the Lord is with thee: blessed art thou among women" (Lk 1:28).

Mary, astonished at the sight of the celestial being, leans back in caution, holds her hand open in surprise, and drops the spindle with which she is working. The heavenly messenger assures Mary that she has no reason to fear and eagerly delivers that incomparable proclamation:

> Behold thou shalt conceive in thy womb, and shalt bring forth a son; and thou shalt call his name Jesus. He shall be great, and shall be called the Son of the most High; and the Lord God shall give unto him the throne of David his father; and he shall reign in the house of Jacob for ever. And of his kingdom there shall be no end (Lk 1:31-33).

Mary responds, "How shall this be done, because I know not man?" (Lk 1:34).

Gabriel explains that "the Holy Ghost shall come upon thee, and the power of the most High shall overshadow thee" (Lk 1:35).

Then, manifesting her deep humility and complete trust in and acceptance of the Divine Will, the Virgin says, "Behold the handmaid of the Lord: be it done to me according to thy word" (Lk 1:38). Mary's striking humility, receptivity, and perfect conformity to the will of God form a preeminent model of Christian behavior for all the faithful.

From the upper center, the blessed and glorious Trinity descends upon Mary in three rays through the action of the Holy Spirit, from a blue semicircle called the *Arc of Heaven*—a representation of that spiritual realm breaking into our earthly existence. At this moment she becomes the *Theotokos*, the Mother of God. For this reason, the Annunciation is also a celebration of the Incarnation of Christ, the God-Man.

Time and Place

The Church believes that Gabriel appeared to Mary in Nazareth, but the icon includes the visual trappings of the Temple of Jerusalem to more effectively draw together its spiritual meanings.

Annunciation uses a technique called *condensed time*, also known as *simultaneous narration*; although the events of the icon occurred in sequence—first, Gabriel's announcement, then the Virgin's acceptance and the conception of Jesus—they are depicted together in the same scene. The icon takes all of these important aspects and presents them simultaneously, not only to capture more significance in a single image but also to emphasize that these events reverberate outside of time and into eternity. Condensed time helps us to liberate our contemplation of the icon from the strict limitations of our temporal existence.

Mary and Gabriel

The Queen of Heaven sits upon two silken, tube-shaped cushions of the type used by members of the Eastern Roman imperial family. We may also note that her footrest is higher than Gabriel's, indicating her greater status. Mary's royalty is obvious: that a human being could have an honor surpassing that of the angels themselves—namely, the privilege of being the Mother of God—is a marvel of such surpassing glory that we may never fully understand it in this life or the next.

Mary's spindle is a reference to the *Protoevangelion of James*, which records that she was assigned the duty of spinning the purple and red veil for the Temple. The veil itself is directly behind Our Lady, set between simplified versions of the Temple's pillars, and in this image it is blue so that there is adequate visual contrast between Mary and the veil.

Later, both the fruit of Mary's womb, Christ, and the work of Mary's hands, the veil, are rent during the Crucifixion (Mt 27:51). Regardless of whether the Theotokos actually did weave the veil, this iconographic detail conveys both her willingness to become the Mother of God and the ultimate mission of her divine Offspring.

The archangel's depiction befits a messenger from the heavenly court—a clavus of rank on his arm, an ornately curled courtly hairstyle, and a messenger's staff. His fingers are arranged in a position that conveys a proclamation.

Feast Day - March 25:
The Annunciation of Our Most Holy Lady, the Mother of God and Ever-Virgin Mary

Troparion, Tone IV:
Today is the crown of our salvation, * and the unfolding of the eternal mystery; * the Son of God becomes the Virgin's Son, * and Gabriel brings the good tidings of grace. * With him let us also cry to the Mother of God: * Rejoice, Full of grace! The Lord is with you.

Dormition of the Mother of God

"Dormition" means "falling asleep" and is one way by which Scripture often expresses the death of a holy person. Although the death of Mary is not recorded in Holy Writ, the Church remembers her passing with the same language of honor.

The body of our blessed and glorious Lady rests on an imperial pillow atop a funeral bed.

From a glorious three-tiered mandorla, Christ receives her soul, now newly born into heaven. In a reversal of their typical portrayals, the God-Man is the Parent who holds His child. The swaddling clothes resemble a burial shroud, reminding us that death in this world leads to life anew in the next.

Mary's monogram now appears around her soul, her more essential self, rather than her body. A six-winged fiery seraph flies above, escorting the Queen of Heaven (Lk 1:32; Apoc 12) to her new kingdom.

Apostles and first-century bishops bow to her in veneration, and many show their remorse. In the foreground, Peter censes her and Paul covers his hands in reverence.

A beardless John, Mary's adopted son by Our Lord's command (Jn 19:26), stands at the foot of the bed to the far right, ready to carry the body to the tomb and watch over it for three days, according to the burial custom of the time.

Time and Place, and the Honor of Mary

The arched doorway on a pointed building, to the right, is an abstracted image of the Temple and tells us that the action is in Jerusalem.

Although the Bible itself does not discuss this event, we have the reliable testimony of credible witnesses, passed down by holy tradition and recorded by the Fathers of the Church, and the celebration has been kept by Christians of the Near East from the earliest centuries AD.

Besides simply honoring the date of the Mother of God's death, as with other saints, on this day the Church celebrates how Mary, being without any spot of sin, was received into heaven body and soul; we rejoice in the glory and honor that God thus bestowed upon her. *Dormition* also reminds us that what Mary experienced is waiting for all of us at the end of time in the General Resurrection, when all souls will be reunited with their bodies.

The censer conveys the sanctity of Mary, and it is also a type of her womb, which held Christ, the divine Coal from heaven. God foreshadowed this through Isaias, who—in a prefigurement of the Eucharist—received a burning coal to remove his sins (Is 6:6-7). The prophet received the "live coal" from tongs, and Our Lady is in a certain sense the tongs by which the Father delivered His Son to our world. We commemorate all of this during the Divine Liturgy, when after all who come forth have received the Holy Eucharist, the priest recites a version of what the angel said to Isaias: "This hath touched thy lips, and thy iniquities shall be taken away, and thy sin shall be cleansed" (Is 6:7).

Christ and the Seraph

The Mighty One often wears robes of glorious orange after His Resurrection; this fiery hue combines the colors and significations of red and gold and thus radiantly exalts Him as "the first begotten of the dead, and the prince of the kings of the earth" (Apoc 1:5).

A seraph is present—one from the rank of angels that smoulders with love for God and sing His glory without end. He burns with a fiery red that captures his ardent passion for his Creator. Isaias thus describes his vision of seraphim:

> I saw the Lord sitting upon a throne high and elevated: and his train filled the temple. Upon it stood the seraphims: the one had six wings, and the other had six wings: with two they covered his face, and with two they covered his feet, and with two they flew. And they cried one to another, and said: Holy, holy, holy, the Lord God of hosts, all the earth is full of his glory (Is 6:1-3).

Feast Day - August 15:
The Dormition of Our Most Holy Lady, the Mother of God and Ever-Virgin Mary

Kontakion, Tone II:
The tomb and death could not hold the Mother of God, * unceasing in her intercession and an unfailing hope of patronage, * for, as the Mother of Life she was transferred to life * by Him Who had dwelt in her ever-virgin womb.

Apostles and Bishops

The presence of the Apostles, the human foundations of our Church, indicates how highly the Church honors the Mother of God.

The two bishops, identifiable by their cross-emblazoned omophoria, are first-century figures, formerly judges of the Athenian Areopagus converted by Paul: Hierotheus, left, and Dionysius. The latter is mentioned in the Acts of the Apostles (17:34); there is some question as to whether the former actually existed, but the Church in her wisdom continues to honor his memory in the calendar of saints.

By their presence, together with the Apostles, we are shown in a small space that all of the members of the Body of Christ share in honoring Our Lady.

According to pious tradition, Thomas was late and did not reach Mary's bedside while she was alive; rather, assisted by an angel, he arrived after the funeral rites were over. The Apostle yearned to reverence Our Lady, so they opened the tomb for him, and her body was missing—only a strong, pleasing aroma was present. In this way the early faithful learned of the bodily resurrection of the Virgin.

Matthias

Thomas' tardiness does provide an opportunity for the rarely depicted and underappreciated Matthias to make an appearance. Although there were in total fourteen men who were called Apostles at one time or another, they are preferably shown as a group of twelve to remind the viewer that they were foreshadowed by the twelve sons of Jacob and thus also by the Twelve Tribes of Israel. When the Apostles are depicted before the Crucifixion, Judas is among them. Matthias was chosen to replace the traitorous one (Acts 1:23-26); nevertheless, when a scene takes place after the Crucifixion, Matthias is normally replaced by the more noteworthy Paul, Apostle to the Gentiles (Rom 11:13; 2 Tm 1:11).

Matthias is unique in being the only Apostle not personally chosen by Christ; as such, he is the first example of *apostolic succession*, that continuation of the office of the Apostles through all the bishops of the world, one generation after the next, in an unbroken line to the present day and until the end of the world.

Matthias is usually portrayed as an old man, frequently with a moderate-to-long white beard, but his features are less fixed than those of the other Apostles because he is so rarely included.

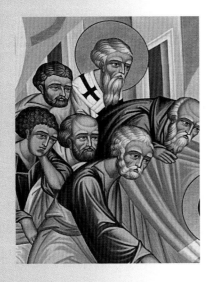

Feast Day - August 9:

Kontakion, Tone IV:
Your radiant message, O wondrous apostle Matthias, * has shone like the sun throughout the world * enlightening the Church of the nations with grace.

Holy Meeting of the Lord in the Temple

This icon is also known as *Presentation of the Lord in the Temple.*

Mary and Joseph bring the forty-day-old Christ to the Temple of Jerusalem to fulfill the Mosaic Law regarding the "sanctification of the first-born" (Lk 2:23; Ex 13:2). Everyone in this icon prayerfully performs the actions prescribed for them by the Old Law.

The Holy Prophet and God-Receiver Simeon descends the stairs from where the Loaves of Proposition are kept, and the Mother of God, hands veiled, bows and gives the Child to him—for God had promised Simeon that he would not die before he had seen the Christ (Lk 2:26). He receives the Savior in his covered arms and recognizes that he may now die in peace, because "my eyes have seen thy salvation, Which thou hast prepared before the face of all peoples: A light to the revelation of the Gentiles, and the glory of thy people Israel" (Lk 2:30-32).

Simeon blesses them, then he foretells that Christ and Mary will suffer but that glory will come forth from this suffering: "Behold this child is set for the fall, and for the resurrection of many in Israel, and for a sign which shall be contradicted; And thy own soul a sword shall pierce, that, out of many hearts, thoughts may be revealed" (Lk 2:34-35).

Joseph, hands veiled, holds two turtle doves, the offering expected by the Temple from those who could not afford a lamb (Lk 2:24; Lv 12:6-8).

The Holy Prophetess Anna recognizes that Jesus is the Christ; she indicates Our Lord with a teaching gesture and speaks of Him "to all that looked for the redemption of Israel" (Lk 2:36-38).

Feast Day - February 2:
The Meeting of Our Lord,
God, and Savior, Jesus Christ

Troparion, Tone I:
Rejoice, full of grace, Virgin
Mother of God! * From you
there dawned the Sun of
Righteousness, Christ our God,
* Who enlightens those who
dwell in darkness. * And you,
O righteous Elder, be glad! *
You received in your embrace
* the Liberator of our souls, *
Who grants us resurrection.

Great and Holy Friday -
Descent from the Cross:

Troparion, Tone IV (HT):
Thou hast redeemed us
from the curse of the Law
by Thy precious Blood.
* By being nailed to the
Cross and pierced with the
Spear, * Thou hast poured
immortality on mankind. *
O our Savior, glory to Thee.

Christ

Christ is clothed in the resplendent orange that is usually reserved for Him after the Resurrection as an expression of His luminous glory; here it is used to distinguish Him visually from the Mother of God, with whom He typically shares the blue and red color scheme.

Two pedestals of honor are atop one another—one for Our Lord, and one for Simeon. This is necessary because of their physical proximity and the need for Christ to have His own pedestal.

Simeon and Anna

Simeon and Anna represent the "fullness of time," that is, the belief that those who wait patiently for God's plans to unfold are rewarded. The feast is a profound link between the promises of the Old Testament and their fulfillment in the New.

The old age of prophet and prophetess is evident in their sunken cheekbones. Their advanced years and Simeon's willingness to be "dismissed" by God, now that he has seen the Savior, foretells that the Mosaic Law has lived out its useful lifespan (Heb 8:13; Zac 11:6-10) and is in its final moments before Christ replaces it with the law of love (Mt 22:37).

Simeon the God-Receiver leans in affectionately toward Christ, his hands veiled in respect for the great Majesty he is holding and his face showing the sorrow that he now feels having foreseen what the Christ will have to endure.

Anna holds a scroll that indicates her status as a prophetess.

The Temple; Christ's Sacrifice Prefigured

The Temple is represented in the background by an altar covered by a liturgical canopy called a *ciborium* supported by four marble columns. It is draped by the usual red fabric swag to convey that the scene takes place indoors, or at least under a portico and not in the courtyard.

Joseph's doves recall Christ's death for ours sins—His holy oblation, of which these birds and other sacrificial animals of the Old Covenant are a vivid type. In the image, Christ the Lamb of God (Jn 1:29; Lv 12:6) is physically closer to the Temple than the doves, and thus He supplants them as the true and final sacrifice "for the destruction of sin" (Heb 9:26).

Another symbol of the Eucharist is indirectly represented—the stairs lead to the Loaves of Proposition, that is, the twelve loaves of bread that were continually left in the Tabernacle or the Temple under the Mosaic Law as an offering to God (Ex 25:30). The old loaves would be consumed by the ritually clean priests on the Sabbath as "an atoning sacrifice" (Ex 29:32) and replaced with fresh loaves.

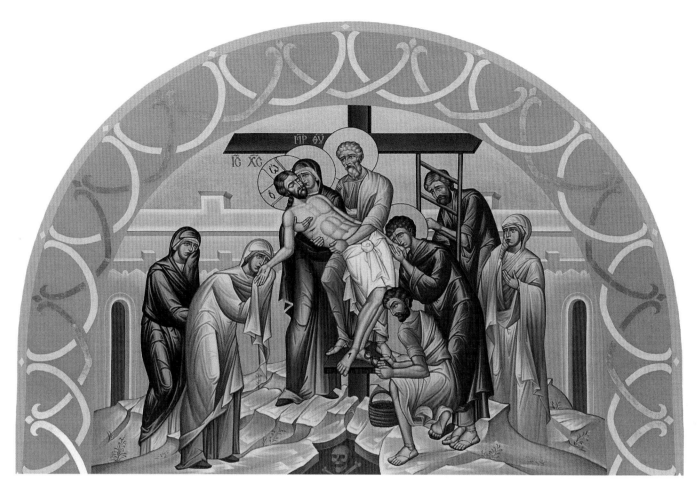

Descent from the Cross

Christ's suffering is over, but those who remain on Calvary have much sorrow left to bear.

Joseph of Arimathea, who will bury Christ in his own tomb (Mt 27:60), hands His body over to Our Lady, who lovingly cradles Him and presses her face to His. Nicodemus—Pharisee, member of the Sanhedrin, and devoted follower of Christ (Jn 3) who later helped to place Him in the tomb (Jn 19:39-40)—leans mournfully against a ladder.

The beloved disciple John, present on Calvary during the Crucifixion (Jn 19:35), adores His left hand; Mary Magdalene (Mt 27:56), her own hands veiled, sobs into His right hand. Behind her, Mary the wife of Cleopas, (Mt 27:56) mother of James, uses her robe to wipe away tears.

To the far right, Salome, who watched from afar (Mk 15:40), gestures in disbelief at what has happened to the Son of God.

Another disciple removes the nails from His feet, saving the precious relics in a small basket.

Christ and Golgotha

Our Lord's body is of a greenish pallor, indicating that His soul and divinity are now gone and are in *Hades*, the abode of the dead, where He proclaims the Good News to the righteous departed (1 Pt 3:19-20) and frees them from their exile from God (Eph 4:8). Our Lord bears the wounds of the nails and lance, and the weight of His body is supported by a *suppadaneum*, the foot block attached to the cross.

The walls of Jerusalem in the background place the scene outside of Jerusalem. The calves and goats sacrificed for sin under the Old Law were carried "without the camp" (Lv 16:27), and likewise Christ was sacrificed beyond the walls of the holy city.

Defeated Hades is represented by a black cave below the conquering Redeemer's feet, and the gap in the rock also calls to mind the earthquake that rent the land upon Christ's death (Mt 27:51).

The crucifixion takes place on the hill Golgotha (Jn 19:17), Hebrew for "place of the skull," and the viewer is reminded of its name by the skull and crossbones at the bottom of the image. According to pious tradition, these remains belong to Adam, such that Christ was crucified on the spot where the first man was buried. In other words, the New Adam conquered death where the Old Adam suffered it, and Christ now descends into the blackness and death of Hades to rescue Adam and his children.

Mark's Gospel (15:22) notes that Golgotha "being interpreted is, The place of Calvary." This other name is from the Latin word for skull, *calveria*.

Fresh sprigs of greenery represent the new life and regeneration that are bestowed upon the world by Christ's redemptive sacrifice and victory over death. Greenery is also a common motif related to the unspoiled paradise of Eden before the Fall of Man, and thus in this image it symbolizes our return to friendship with God.

Joseph and Nicodemus ... and Nicodemus?

Joseph of Arimathea, a wealthy follower of Our Lord who donated his tomb to Him, is adorned with a clavus of rank and classical curled hair.

Four of Christ's eight followers lack nimbi, probably as a result of artistic constraints. Although the Mother of God and John are clearly of higher order than the others, Joseph's nimbus does not here imply that he is of greater holiness than the other disciples.

At first glance, there appear to be two Nicodemi here. Typically, in *Descent* icons Nicodemus is pulling the nails from Christ's feet, and in another icon called *Deposition* or *Lamentation* Nicodemus is leaning upon a ladder. Given the attention to detail on the upper figure, versus the less-detailed profile of the lower figure, it is probable that the man near the ladder is intended to be Nicodemus.

The sandal is falling off the foot of the man extracting the nails; this is usually a sign of shock, but here it primarily indicates profound remorse. Nevertheless, this feature is uncommon in *Descent* icons and thus may be an example of a motif creeping in where it once was not.

Veneration of Relics

It is not surprising that the early Christians would wish to save Christ's nails, for it is deeply human to hold on to something connected to a lost loved one. To apply this profound impulse to the God-Man is only right and proper.

Furthermore, the Jews knew of instances in which relics effected miraculous healing (4 Kgs 13:20-21), and they recognized the worth of holy items belonging to great figures such as Elias (4 Kgs 2:11-15) and Aaron (Heb 9:4). Similarly, after the Crucifixion, wonders were wrought through Paul's handkerchiefs and aprons, independent of the presence of Paul himself (Acts 19:11-12). Indeed, the body is the temple of the Holy Spirit (1 Cor 3:16), and the grace of God may continue to work through not only the body but also items that were close to it.

Myrrh-Bearing Women

Very early in the morning, "the sun now being risen" (Mk 16:2), three of the Lord's female disciples—Mary Magdalene, Joanna, and Mary of Cleopas (Lk 24:10)—bring ointments and spices to His tomb to complete the process of burial (Lk 24:1).

Then, "Behold there was a great earthquake. For an angel of the Lord descended from heaven, and coming, rolled back the stone, and sat upon it. And his countenance was as lightning, and his raiment as snow" (Mt 28:2-3). The leftmost angel's wings point upward, suggesting his rush downward to meet the women.

Astonished, the three mourners draw back at the sight of the celestial beings. One pinches up her cloak in fear.

The angels know that the women seek the body of Jesus; the central messenger motions to the sepulcher and says, "He is not here, for he is risen, as he said. Come, and see the place where the Lord was laid" (Mt 28:6). Our Lord's body is no longer there, and His burial shroud lies empty, neither uncut nor unwrapped.

Resurrection Motifs

The sprigs of greenery are larger than in *Descent from the Cross*, showing that humanity's new spiritual regeneration continues to take root and grow, drawing strength from the unquenchable grace flowing from the Resurrection.

Feast Day:
Sunday of the Myrrh-
Bearing Women -
Third Sunday of Pascha

Kontakion, Tone II:
You commanded the myrrh-
bearers to rejoice, O Christ
God, * and ended the grief
of our mother Eve by Your
resurrection. * You ordered
the apostles to proclaim
to all: * "The Savior is
risen from the tomb."

Christ's burial shroud is unbroken, demonstrating that He did not physically "escape" from the wrappings or cut through them, and therefore He could not have faked His death nor did His followers fake His resurrection. The unbroken shroud also recalls the tomb that Christ left while still sealed by the stone (Mt 28:1-6), the Mother of God's unopened womb (Mt 1:23; Ez 44:1-2), and the unopened door to the upper room (Jn 20:19).

Hierarchical Composition

Myrrh-Bearing Women may be read from right to left, in increasing holiness— the small cave, then saintly human beings, and then the heavenly creatures with the tomb and burial implements of Our Lord.

The cave behind the women symbolizes the old life of darkness and death that afflicted humanity before Christ's redemptive sacrifice, but which is now left behind. This cave is both smaller and less central to the image than the actual tomb from which Christ our Light emerged.

The icon may also be read as a spiritual ascent from bottom to top—the highest point of the cave of darkness is lower than the human beings; the angel's raised wings place him above the women; and above all is Christ's most glorious cross on Golgotha.

Women

The Gospels recount that Mary Magdalene, Salome, Joanna, and Mary the wife of Cleopas visited Our Lord's tomb. Tradition holds that Mary and Martha of Bethany, the sisters of Lazarus, and Susanna were there as well.

How can we determine the identities of these women? Scripture several times mentions disciples meeting angels after the Resurrection, and it appears that this icon uses Luke's Gospel, as it is the only version that explicitly mentions two angels. Thus, the viewer can know that these three women are Mary Magdalene, Joanna, and Mary the wife of Cleopas, also known as the mother of James.

Golgotha

The site of the Crucifixion is visible in the background. To Christ's right hung the good thief, traditionally known as St. Dismas, and to His left was the thief who abused Him, Gestas (Lk 23:39-43).

Comparing Golgotha in this image to the depiction of it in *Descent from the Cross*, we can deduce from the peak of the hill being behind the cross, and also from the ladder leaning on the back of the cross, that we are viewing the "front side," where Our Lord and the thieves would have hung.

Descent of the Holy Spirit

This feast day is also commonly known as Pentecost, because it occurred at the end of that Jewish celebration (Acts 2:1), which was itself a type and shadow of the Descent of the Holy Spirit. But the Jewish feast of Pentecost is not what the day commemorates.

The Apostles were hiding "for fear of the Jews" (Jn 20:19) in an upper room in Jerusalem (Acts 1:12), and "suddenly there came a sound from heaven, as of a mighty wind coming, and it filled the whole house where they were sitting" (Acts 2:2).

Here, from the Arc of Heaven, "There appeared to them parted tongues as it were of fire, and it sat upon every one of them: And they were all filled with the Holy Ghost, and they began to speak with divers tongues, according as the Holy Ghost gave them to speak" (Acts 2:3-4).

An aged king named Cosmos—a personification of fallen humanity, which was originally the crown of God's physical creation but now is grown old in sin and dwells in darkness—stands outside of the room and awaits the Apostles' Good News, represented by the twelve scrolls that he holds.

Immediately after the Holy Spirit descends upon them, the Apostles—all of whom were from Galilee—preach to devout Jews from every nation visiting Jerusalem:

Kontakion, Tone VIII:
When the Most High
came down and confused
the tongues, * He parted
the nations. * When He
divided the tongues of fire,
* He called all to unity;*
thus with one voice * we
glorify the all-Holy Spirit.

Parthians, and Medes, and Elamites, and inhabitants of Mesopotamia, Judea, and Cappadocia, Pontus and Asia, Phrygia, and Pamphylia, Egypt, and the parts of Libya about Cyrene, and strangers of Rome, Jews also, and proselytes, Cretes, and Arabians: we have heard them speak in our own tongues the wonderful works of God (Acts 2:9-11).

Between Peter and Paul is a space reserved for Christ, invisibly present.

The Holy Spirit

The Descent of the Holy Spirit is the birthday of the Church, and as a sign of the fullness of the institution of the Church, all following Sundays until Great Lent are numbered as "Sundays after Pentecost." The day is also a glorious celebration of the Holy Spirit.

The composition of the icon reflects the *Mystical Supper*, another event during which the Apostles received an intimate gift of communion with God.

The Apostles

The Apostles hold scrolls representing the Word of God, which they will transmit to the world. Where their right arms are visible, we can see clavi indicating their high status.

Peter and Paul, the Apostles of Rome and the pillars of the Church, are always seated together in the middle. Peter is especially honored, as we see in his traditional golden yellow clothing.

While Paul was not yet an Apostle during the historical Descent, he is shown here in another example of condensed time, for he would later become an Apostle equal to, if not greater than, the others (Acts 2). Also, the Prophet Joel proclaimed that the Holy Spirit would come upon the whole Church (Jl 2:28), and this is another reason for including in the image a person who was not actually present.

Cosmos

Although the blackness in which he stands appears to be on the floor, this is actually a stylized door—that is, a door to the Upper Room; it separates the terrified Apostles from the outside world, but soon they will burst through it in order to bring humanity back into friendship with God.

Cosmos is dressed as an emperor of Constantinople; around his body he wears a type of jeweled stole called a *loros*. He holds the twelve scrolls of the Apostles, which contain the saving doctrine that he will soon embrace.

The name "Cosmos" is a transliteration of a Greek word that originally meant "good order" or "orderly arrangement"; this name reminds us that before the Fall, both man and the created order were things of perfection and beauty: "They were very good" (Gn 1:31).

Unity in Diversity

Now the confusion of tongues that God wrought at Babel is undone; all nations and languages may reunite in the Church's bosom.

But unity of purpose and belief does not suggest uniformity. The same Fire comes for all, but a different Tongue rests upon each person. In the image, no bodily posture or color scheme is perfectly repeated among the Twelve. As Paul says, "There are diversities of graces, but the same Spirit; And there are diversities of ministries, but the same Lord; And there are diversities of operations, but the same God, who worketh all in all" (1 Cor 12:4-6). Similarly, each individual Catholic and all of the different rites within the Catholic Church have diverse gifts that should be preserved and fostered.

It is interesting to contrast the serene *Descent* with the confusion of *Ascension*, where the Apostles, yet to receive the fullness of the Holy Spirit, were truly bewildered. In this icon, everyone is calmly seated despite the overwhelming power of God that has come upon them. Only a few sandals falling off signal the astonishment that would naturally arise during such a sublime manifestation of God's presence. Though some unbelievers mistook their zeal for drunkenness (Acts 2:13-15), the image reminds us that the movements of the Spirit are orderly and do not produce frenzied or delirious ecstasies.

Undoing the Confusion of Tongues

For approximately the first eighteen hundred years of man's existence, our ancestors spoke the same language (Gn 11:1). But then the great mass of humanity attempted to build a tower to reach heaven; the Lord, seeing their pride, said, "Let us go down, and there confound their tongue, that they may not understand one another's speech. And so the Lord scattered them from that place into all lands, and they ceased to build the city" (Gn 11:7-8).

In the early centuries after Christ, the gift of tongues made it clear that the separation of the nations and languages was undone in the Church and that humanity was reunited in Christ. Also, in the Apostolic Era there were not yet copies of the Gospels in all languages nor native speakers ready to proclaim it to the disparate tribes of humanity, and thus the gift of tongues assisted the Church's missionary efforts.

It is important to note the distinction between the gift of tongues given to the Apostles on Pentecost—called *xenolalia*, the ability to speak in a foreign language that one does not know, such that others may understand—and "tongues" as practiced in other contexts. The latter is known as *glossolalia* and consists of ecstatic utterances of no known language and not intelligible to the listener without a gift of interpretation (1 Cor 14:27).

The Apostle Paul provided much precise guidance about tongues.

It is a lesser gift than prophecy (1 Cor 14:3,19) and is far down the list of the gifts of the Holy Spirit (1 Cor 12), and the saint beseeches Christians to "be zealous for the better gifts" (1 Cor 12:31). Tongues are not even mentioned in lists of the gifts later in the New Testament, such as in Romans 12, Galatians 5, Ephesians 4, 1 Timothy 4, 2 Timothy 1, and 1 Peter 4.

Because God is not the author of confusion (1 Cor 14:33), when tongues are practiced such that no listener can understand, it is not helpful in teaching others the Gospel of Christ (1 Cor 14:19); it is at *best* for personal edification (1 Cor 14:4) and is in some ways a re-confusing of the languages. Speaking in tongues should be for the benefit of the listeners (1 Cor 14:5,26), and if the tongues cannot be understood the speaker should be silent (1 Cor 14:28).

Indeed, the Apostle notes that confused tongues may be a sign of unbelief and impending judgment (1 Cor 14:21), and he quotes from Isaias, who prophesied that the Lord would speak to Israel in a language that they did not understand before they were destroyed by the Assyrians (Is 28:11-14; Dt 28:49-50).

Thus, when Paul says that confused tongues are a sign for unbelievers (1 Cor 14:22), he means the speakers themselves; for this same reason Christ spoke in parables—as a punishment to those without faith, who would not understand Him (Mt 13:11-15).

The Apostle declares that "tongues shall cease" (1 Cor 13:8), and—besides rare instances among extraordinary saints—the gift of xenolalia has been absent since the early centuries of the Church.

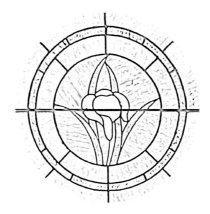

Chapter 5:
Wall Feasts and Scenes

Of old, God the incorporeal and uncircumscribed was never depicted. Now, however, when God is seen clothed in flesh, and conversing with men, I make an image of the God whom I see. I do not worship matter, I worship the God of matter, who became matter for my sake, and deigned to inhabit matter, who worked out my salvation through matter. I will not cease from honoring that matter which works my salvation.

**-St. John of Damascus
Apologia Against Those Who Decry Holy Images, circa AD 729**

Biblical Scenes

In the following text, the icons are presented in chronological order, though at the time of this writing they are not displayed in this order in the church.

In general, the first six icons depict events in the earlier days of Christ's ministry, starting with His first public miracle during the wedding feast at Cana. The second six concern the events preceding and continuing through Christ's Passion, starting with *Raising of Lazarus* and ending with *Anastasis*, His victory over death.

This cycle of icons is closely bound together by the iconographer's style, attention to detail, Ukrainian titling, and aesthetic uniformity.

Even when effort is made to distinguish between the Apostles, the traditional identifying features are typically ignored, except with Peter, who exhibits some degree of consistency. Judas is here-and-there indicated by his sour expression.

Also notably different in these images are the personal details: with rare exceptions, the figures lack the Late Antique trappings of dress and hairstyle, and their faces do not have the look of classical portraiture seen in most of the other icons in the church. Rather, they are usually more severe, with heavy, serious brows, angular features, and functional medieval Eastern European haircuts.

Much effort was made to compose these icons such that they not only retell the events but also include meaningful details, such as Martha's jar of perfume in *Raising of Lazarus*. Also, secondary events that took place immediately before or after the main scene are here and there included, and these add many layers of theological meaning.

Although these icons are not always as immediately bold and eye-catching as some of the other works in the church, the author must express his special appreciation for them—they preserve many traditions yet have their own unique personality, all the while reverberating with uncommon richness and detail.

Nativity of Our Lord

This icon is entitled in Ukrainian РІЗДВО ІСУСА ХРИСТА—"The Nativity of Jesus Christ."

Joseph and the pregnant Virgin travel from Galilee, their city of residence, to Bethlehem, the city of their fathers of the stock of King David, to be enrolled in the census declared by the Roman Emperor Augustus.

"It came to pass, that when they were there, her days were accomplished, that she should be delivered. And she brought forth her firstborn son, and wrapped him up in swaddling clothes, and laid him in a manger; because there was no room for them in the inn" (Lk 2:6-7).

Shepherds watch their flocks nearby, and "Behold an angel of the Lord stood by them, and the brightness of God shone round about them; and they feared with a great fear. And the angel said to them: Fear not; for, behold, I bring you good tidings of great joy, that shall be to all the people: For, this day, is born to you a Savior, who is Christ the Lord, in the city of David" (Lk 2:9-11). Thereafter, a great multitude of angels appeared and praised God, saying, "Glory to God in the highest; and on earth peace to men of good will" (Lk 2:13).

One shepherd plays a reed pipe, joining human music to the song of the heavenly army.

Just above Christ, from the Arc of Heaven, a ray of light marks the course of the Star of Bethlehem, from which certain wise men from the East discern the birth of Christ.

Those wise men approach King Herod to inquire about the location of the favored Child. Herod, jealous of a potential rival, pretends that he also wishes to reverence Christ and asks the wise men to find out where He is and return to him:

> Who having heard the king, went their way; and behold the star which they had seen in the east, went before them, until it came and stood over where the child was. And seeing the star they rejoiced with exceeding great joy. And entering into the house, they found the child with Mary his mother, and falling down they adored him; and opening their treasures, they offered him gifts; gold, frankincense, and myrrh. And having received an answer in sleep that they should not return to Herod, they went back another way into their country (Mt 2:9-12).

In an example of simultaneous narration, to the lower right midwives bathe the Holy Child.

Christ and Mary

The Son of God and His mother are much larger than the other figures; this conveys their importance, in another instance of hierarchical perspective.

Many elements in *Nativity* prefigure Christ's sacrifice. The Child wears the traditional shroud-like swaddling clothes, and He is laid in a manger (Lk 2:7) shaped like a crypt; these details teach us that Christ was born into this world to die and remind us of the connection between death and new life. The word "manger" is sometimes misunderstood to mean "stable," but a manger is actually a feeding trough. We can only marvel at God's sublime poetry—the Bread of Life (Jn 6:35) is born into a feeding trough, for through His real presence in the Holy Eucharist He will be food for our souls and bodies.

Christ the Light (Jn 1:1-15) is brought forth into the darkness of a cave, which recalls this world of sin and death and which visually connects His birth with the cave in which He will later be buried. The *Protoevangelion of James* mentions a mountain grotto, and early Christian tradition places the manger in a cave; indeed, the Church of the Nativity, first built in AD 327, is constructed over what is believed to be the actual cave. As early as the second century, St. Justin Martyr mentioned the cave in his *Dialogue with Trypho*.

The large, red, imperial silken pillow emphasizes the Virgin's royalty and evokes that she is the fulfillment of the Old Testament type of the Burning Bush, from the midst of which the Lord spoke to Moses. Flames radiated from the bush but it was not consumed (Ex 3:1-4), and likewise the Holy Virgin brought forth Christ the Light yet remained untouched by the fires of sensuality. The sinless Mary reclines peacefully to show that she had no pain in childbirth, thus reversing the curse of the disobedient Eve (Gn 3:16). Peacefully the Queen bestows a loving glance upon her husband Joseph, looking much beleaguered from the stress of the events surrounding the birth.

The Ox and Ass

Behind them, a donkey and an ox gaze at the King. These animals were first mentioned in the apocryphal *Gospel of Pseudo-Matthew* and have found their way into the iconographic tradition for their rich biblical significance.

The pair symbolize the Jews and pagan Gentiles who watch the birth in wonder. The Jews are represented by the ox, a working animal, for the Jews labor under the yoke of the Old Law. The Gentiles, who do not participate in the Mosaic covenant, are represented by the donkey, an unclean animal according to the prescriptions of the Old Law (Lv 11:1-8). The ox and ass also recall a prophecy of Isaias (1:3): "The ox knoweth his owner, and the ass his master's crib: but Israel hath not known me, and my people hath not understood." In other words, not all of Israel will accept the Christ, and His Church will be formed from a mixture of Jews and Gentiles.

Joseph and the Old Man

The foster-father of Our Lord is depicted on a smaller scale and somewhat distant from the birth, emphasizing that his flesh did not father the Child.

The Adversary, old with sin and dressed in goat skins as the old pagan god Pan, is tempting Joseph to doubt the miracle that he has just witnessed. If someone so saintly and close to God had trials of faith, we must also expect them.

Angels and Shepherds

Besides representing the celebration of the entire angelic host, the three angels betoken the presence of the Holy Trinity.

Feast Day - December 25:
The Nativity According-to-the-Flesh of Our Lord, God, and Savior Jesus Christ

Troparion, Tone IV:
Your Nativity, O Christ our God, * made the light of knowledge dawn on the world; * through it, those who worshipped the stars were taught by a star * to worship You, the Sun of Righteousness, * and to know You, the Dawn from on high.[9] * Glory to You, O Lord.

[9] The more literal translation used in other versions reads, "Those who worship the stars * have been taught by a star to worship Thee, * the Sun of righteousness, * and to know Thee *the Orient* from on high" (*HT*; cf. *SB*; emphasis added). This is a theologically and scripturally important concept. See Zacharias 3:8 and 6:12, and also Luke 1:78.

The shepherds are the Jews in the scene, welcoming the birth of their Messiah. Atypically for Jews in iconography, instead of sandals they wear leggings, which signify their life of rural labors. One of their lambs is trapped in thorns, recalling a well-known type of Christ—namely, the "ram amongst the briers" (Gn 22:13) that God allowed Abraham to sacrifice in place of his son Isaac. Similarly, the Lamb of God (Jn 1:29) will be sacrificed so that we may be spared the eternal death of hell.

Magi

The Magi approach the star, hands covered, bearing gifts. They wear Persian caps and the silk robes of their profession.

They are of a priestly class from a society east of Israel, most likely Persia, and they probably practiced Zoroastrianism or a similar pagan religion. The word *magi* is the plural form of the word *magus*, from a Greek word indicating a person involved in astrology, dream interpretation, and similar occult practices.

They are also called "wise men" (Mt 2:1), not necessarily because they were wise by the standards of the evangelists but because this term was traditionally used in the Old Testament for those versed in pagan learning and ritual.

What they were not, however, were kings. That belief is derived from speculation that they are the kings mentioned in Isaias 60:3 or Psalm 71:11. Yet none of the Church Fathers refer to them as kings. In this icon, they represent the finding of Christ by the Gentile nations.

Although the actual number of magi is not recorded in Scripture, three are traditionally depicted in accordance with the number of gifts mentioned in the Gospel. They also mirror the trio of myrrh-bearing women who brought "spices and ointments" (Lk 23:56) to Christ after His death.

Their three gifts have specific meanings: gold, to honor Christ's kingship; frankincense, to worship His divinity; and myrrh, a spice used during burial, to foretell His glorious death.

Midwives

The two ladies to the lower right represent another detail taken from the *Protoevangelion of James*.

One, named Zelomi, pours bathwater for the newborn Christ and tests its temperature with her hand. Her washbasin, which will hold the Lord God, is similar to a customary Eastern baptismal font—both are fashioned in the likeness of a Eucharistic chalice. The other, Salome, a first cousin of the Mother of God, is dressed in the pure white raiment of a midwife and cradles Our Lord.

Theophany of Our Lord

The Ukrainian title, БОГОЯВЛЕННЯ ГОСПОДНЕ, translates roughly to "Our Lord's Revelation of Himself." This meaning is conveyed by the English word "theophany," which is from the Greek for "an appearance of God."

John the Forerunner, the last of the prophets of the Old Covenant, is in the desert preaching repentance and penance and baptizing in the Jordan River.

The people, left, being much impressed, think that John might be the promised savior. But he dismisses this, saying, "There cometh after me one mightier than I, the latchet of whose shoes I am not worthy to stoop down and loose. I have baptized you with water; but he shall baptize you with the Holy Ghost" (Mk 1:7-8).

Christ approaches John to be baptized, but John, whose countenance expresses his feelings of unworthiness, stops him, saying, "I ought to be baptized by thee, and comest thou to me? And Jesus answering, said to him: Suffer it to be so now. For so it becometh us to fulfill all justice" (Mt 3:14-15).

And so the last of the prophets baptizes the Messiah.

Christ's right hand points downward, blessing the Jordan River, and two personifications of the river look back in fear and awe.

Then, "The Holy Ghost descended in a bodily shape, as a dove upon him; and a voice came from heaven: Thou art my beloved Son; in thee I am well pleased" (Lk 3:22).

John's followers, to the left, watch in wonder. To the right, the host of angels bow, their hands veiled in supplication to the Master.

Troparion, Tone I:
When You, O Lord, were
baptized in the Jordan, *
worship of the Trinity was
revealed; * the voice of the
Father bore witness to You, *
naming You the "beloved Son,"
* and the Spirit in the form of
a dove confirmed the Word's
certainty. * Glory to You, O
Christ God, * Who appeared
and enlightened the world.

Christ and Baptism

The Holy One's nakedness recalls the birth of the Old Adam, when he was pure and new.

Christ is without any trace of spot or defect, and thus He did not approach the river seeking forgiveness. Instead, it was an occasion to reveal His glory as a Person of the Trinity and to institute the Catholic mystery of Holy Baptism.

John's baptism is performed in the tradition of the cleansing mentioned in Leviticus 22:4-8, but it also surpasses this cleansing because he calls for repentance, whereas the old washing was simply for ritual purity. John's baptism was a halfway point between the ritualistic cleansing of the Old Covenant and the transforming sacrament of the New, for his baptism did not actually confer grace and remission of sins.

The Holy Spirit and the Jordan

The baptism of Christ receives the title "Theophany" because it is the first overt manifestation of the Trinity. The Father is present in the voice from heaven, the Son is Christ, and the Holy Spirit descends in the form of a dove.

The dove reminds us of the life of Noe, which was itself a prefiguration of baptism. After the waters had drowned the unrighteous, Noe sent forth a dove to look for land, and she came back with an olive branch (Gn 8:11). In this way he learned that dry land was accessible again, but more importantly, that humanity could again thrive upon the earth meant that peace had been restored between God and man. So also here, the dove suggests to us that after Christ's baptism we will soon be restored to God's friendship.

The dove of the Holy Spirit is here mingled with flames, a reference to His descent upon the Apostles in Acts 2. Three rays, signifying the full presence of the Trinity within Him, descend from His *aureole*, another type of full-figure luminous field of holiness.

Two old men, personifications of the Jordan River, pour out the torrent from their jugs. The Jordan is also a symbol for death, and thus it is shown rent in two, for Christ will soon break the gates of Hades. As does Old Man Death in *Anastasis*, the personifications of the Jordan express their shock at the presence of the God-Man.

The Apostle Paul explains the significance of this for Christian baptism:

> Know you not that all we, who are baptized in Christ Jesus, are baptized in his death? For we are buried together with him by baptism into death; that as Christ is risen from the dead by the glory of the Father, so we also may walk in newness of life. For if we have been planted together in the likeness of his death, we shall be also in the likeness of his resurrection (Rom 6:3-5).

The Theophany and the institution of baptism are prefigured several times in Old Testament events involving the Jordan River. Two of the prophets, Elias and Eliseus, divided the Jordan by touching it with the mantle of Elias (4 Kgs 2:8,14), who was a prophetical image of John the Forerunner.

And Josue, a type of Christ, splits the Jordan in Josue 3. Psalm 113 later notes that "Jordan was turned back" by Josue when "Israel went out of Egypt," that is, when God's chosen people left the life of sin associated with the pagan Egyptian nation. Likewise, baptism drowns out the life of sin into which we are born.

John the Forerunner

John's vocation as the last of the prophets of the Old Covenant was the fulfillment of several prophesies. Isaias foretold one who would announce the glory of the Lord and the forgiveness of Jerusalem—"the voice of one crying in the desert: Prepare ye the way of the Lord, make straight in the wilderness the paths of our God" (Is 40:1-5). Israel expected Elias to return as the great harbinger, for the Lord told Malachias, "Behold I will send you Elias the prophet, before the coming of the great and dreadful day of the Lord" (Mal 4:5-6).

Later, after the Forerunner was murdered, Christ explained that he was the prophetical fulfillment of this promise: "Elias is already come, and they knew him not, but have done unto him whatsoever they had a mind" (Mt 17:11-13). John's rough camel-hair robe and his hide belt (the latter not pictured here) (Mt 3:4) identify him as the new Elias, for that great prophet of old was a "hairy man with a girdle of leather about his loins" (4 Kgs 1:8) who lived in the wilderness.

The iconographer included some radiating embellishments in John's nimbus, reminding us that he was a "burning and shining light" (Jn 5:35).

Elias ended his life by passing his prophetical office and hairy cloak to his follower Eliseus (4 Kgs 2:11-15); similarly, in the person of John the Old Law passes away (Lk 16:16) and finds its fulfillment in the New Law and Christ. Although the prophet has not yet died, the Theophany marks the beginning of Jesus' public ministry.

Populace and Tree

A diverse multitude throngs out to see John—Jews and Gentiles, priests and sinners, men and women. Below the crowd of his disciples, a small axe leans expectantly on a tree. When the people approached him, all being sinners—the Pharisees and Sadducees are named in particular—John said to them,

> Ye offspring of vipers, who hath shewed you to flee from the wrath to come? Bring forth therefore fruits worthy of penance; and do not begin to say, We have Abraham for our father. For I say unto you, that God is able of these stones to raise up children to Abraham. For now

Troparion, Tone II:
The just man is remembered with praises, * but for you the Lord's testimony suffices, O Forerunner, * for you truly became more honorable than the prophets * and were deemed worthy to baptize the One foretold. * Then you suffered for the truth and joyfully announced to those in Hades * that God appeared in the flesh, taking away the sin of the world, * and offering us great mercy.

the axe is laid to the root of the trees. Every tree therefore that bringeth not forth good fruit, shall be cut down and cast into the fire (Lk 3:7-9).

The people, now understandably concerned, are eager to know what they must do to be righteous. John replies, "He that hath two coats, let him give to him that hath none; and he that hath meat, let him do in like manner" (Lk 3:11).

To the right, a tax collector (that is, a publican) holds the scales with which he weighs the money he collects. John exhorts the publicans to not collect more from the people than what is due (Lk 3:13).

The third chapter of Matthew's Gospel mentions that *Pharisees* and *Sadducees* were among John's disciples. In the crowd is a man carrying a quill pen, which identifies him as a *scribe*, a professional involved in the interpretation and maintenance of Jewish scriptures and traditions. These individuals were usually Pharisees, a staunchly conservative group who had taken the lead in heroically defending the Jewish religion from pagan influence (1, 2 Mc). Their success in these efforts and the resulting popularity led many of them into pride and self-righteousness.

There is also a priest present; priests were often among the Sadducees, who held the scriptures to be the only binding authority and thus had little respect for tradition. As they were often from priestly families, they had an aristocratic mindset, and they were considered to be too accommodating toward the dominant pagan Greco-Roman culture under which Israel groaned.

He is dressed in the priestly garments described in Exodus 28: a robe with bells and tassels, though no tassels are seen here; a type of linen apron called an *ephod*; and a breastplate, or *hoshen*. The hoshen is inlaid with twelve different jewels inscribed with the names of the Twelve Tribes of Israel. The priest also wears a type of mitre or turban, upon which is a gold plate with the words "Holiness unto YHWH" inscribed in Hebrew.

Roman soldiers also came to the Forerunner to be baptized, and one is included in the image. To them John says, "Do violence to no man; neither calumniate any man; and be content with your pay" (Lk 3:14).

The soldier is composed according to the traditional depiction of St. Longinus, he who pierced Our Lord's heart with a lance—particularly his short rounded gray beard and white cowl over a red cape, but also the Roman scale armor known as *lorica squamata*, leggings, and a shield. We see in *Anastasis* that this same iconographer has clearly intended a similar figure to be Longinus. And so in all likelihood this is him here, though we cannot be perfectly certain.

Adversary

Shortly after Christ was baptized, "The Spirit drove him out into the desert. And he was in the desert forty days and forty nights, and was tempted by Satan; and he was with beasts, and the angels ministered to him" (Mk 1:12-13).

To the upper right, the sour-faced tempter awaits Our Lord, eager to work his vile trickery upon Him. As a fallen angel, he is but a shadow of the beauty of those faithful spirits along the bank of the Jordan. He has bat-like leathern wings and is stooped over, but his head is held high with pride. The blessed angels reflect the glory of the heavenly court, with beautiful, colorful, flowing robes, but the evil one wears a drab, ugly tunic and is an earthy bronze color from head to toe.

Matthew 4 recounts Christ's interactions with this beast.

СВ IВАН ПРЕДТЕЧА

The Wedding at Cana

Gospel Day:
Second Monday of Pascha

Our Lord and Lady attend a wedding celebration at Cana in Galilee, and the supply of wine fails before the guests are satisfied. The Virgin reminds Christ of the thirsty banqueters, but he protests, "Woman, what is that to me and to thee? my hour is not yet come" (Jn 2:4).

But she insists: "His mother saith to the waiters: Whatsoever he shall say to you, do ye" (Jn 2:5). Christ, ever desirous of pleasing His holy mother, calls for six stone water pots, requests that they be filled with water, and then orders that the pots be brought to the chief steward.

The latter, partaking of the drink, "Calleth the bridegroom, And saith to him: Every man at first setteth forth good wine, and when men have well drunk, then that which is worse. But thou hast kept the good wine until now" (Jn 2:9-10).

Peter, at the lead of the Apostles to the left, trembles in fear after witnessing Our Lord's first public miracle. The new spouses express their gratitude, and the guests around the table rejoice for the miraculous vintage.

Canticle of Canticles, 2:1-5
I am the flower of the field, and the lily of the valleys. As the lily among thorns, so is my love among the daughters. As the apple tree among the trees of the woods, so is my beloved among the sons. I sat down under his shadow, whom I desired: and his fruit was sweet to my palate. He brought me into the cellar of wine, he set in order charity in me. Stay me up with flowers, compass me about with apples: because I languish with love.

Composition

The Ukrainian ЩО ЛИШ СКАЖЕ ВАМ, РОБІТЬ! is another translation of Mary's command in verse 5.

Striking is that the Temple of Jerusalem appears in this icon. Cana is far to the north of Jerusalem, and the Temple does not typically appear in *Wedding* icons. However, it is in keeping with the style of this iconographer to include details from immediately before or after the primary event. The Temple's inclusion is therefore likely a foretaste of Christ's next pivotal act according to John 2:14, the cleasing of the Temple—also an icon in this series.

Much simultaneous narration is used—Mary beckons, the servants provide the jars, Christ works the miracle, and the wedding guests exclaim their joy all at the same time. The action occurs indoors, as we know from the hanging swag of fabric.

Christ and Mary, and Theosis

Christ is also a Bridegroom (Mt 9:15), the divine Spouse of the Church; human marriage reflects the mystical marriage between the God-Man and the faithful Catholic, who becomes part of the Body of Christ. As Paul says, "The husband is the head of the wife, as Christ is the head of the church. He is the savior of his body" (Eph 5:23). He further exhorts,

> Husbands, love your wives, as Christ also loved the church, and delivered himself up for it: That he might sanctify it, cleansing it by the laver of water in the word of life: That he might present it to himself a glorious

church, not having spot or wrinkle, or any such thing; but that it should be holy, and without blemish. So also ought men to love their wives as their own bodies. He that loveth his wife, loveth himself. For no man ever hated his own flesh; but nourisheth and cherisheth it, as also Christ doth the church: Because we are members of his body, of his flesh, and of his bones (Eph 5:25-30).

The process that joins the believer to Christ is known as *theosis*, whereby we become "partakers of the divine nature" (2 Pt 1:4). We retain our humanity and are not absorbed into God or transformed into deities; rather, by joining to Him who is like us in all things but sin (Heb 4:15), and who in turn is one with the Father (Jn 17:11, 21-26), we are "strengthened by his Spirit with might unto the inward man" (Eph 3:16) and "filled unto all the fullness of God" (Eph 3:19).

The person who most perfectly fulfills this mystical marriage with Christ is the Mother of God, the Queen of Heaven without stain of sin. Thus, in the icon she represents the entire Church as the bride to whom Christ the Bridegroom is to be united.

Mary, Our Beloved Intercessor

Of all the miracles wrought by Our Lord during His sojourn on earth, this one more than any other was done explicitly to allow its recipients temporal revelry and pleasure.. Besides the spiritual significations, Christ turned the water into wine for the joy of the wedding guests—something extra for their happiness, not solely for their physical or spiritual wholeness.

This miracle of generosity occurred before He even initiated His teaching ministry, and it was done at the behest of His mother whom He loved, and because she loved the wedding guests and desired their joy.

How fervently, then, should we pray to the Mother of God and ask her to entreat her Son on our behalf? For she so clearly loves us, and He so readily listens to her.

Christ the New Wine

Although not depicted in this icon, the chief steward speaks well when he notes that the best wine has been saved for last. Christ is the New Wine, replacing those that came before (Mt 9:17): the Old Covenant and, before it, the less-formal worship offered by the patriarchs from Adam through Noe and by Abram before his calling.

The steward's praise also conveys that Christ is the final and consummate step in salvation history, and that none other shall come after Him.

In another sense, Christ is the New Wine insofar as the miracle is a type of the forthcoming Eucharistic mystery—He changes water to wine as He will later change wine into Himself. For this reason, *Wedding at Cana* is composed such that it is similar in many ways to *Mystical Supper* in this same series.

Groom and Bride, and Guests

On a human level, the miracle underscores Christ's blessing upon marriage, the appropriateness of temperate celebration, and the joy we should find in the ordinary cycles of family life.

One tradition indicates that at least one of the two spouses was a relative of the Holy Family.

The bride and groom wear crowns and drink from a common cup, details taken from the Greek Catholic marriage ceremony—the Office of Crowning. The crowns signify the new kingdom that they will share and lead in their household, and it also echoes Christ's crown of thorns—for the spouses must sacrifice themselves for one another. The cup does not contain the Eucharist but rather blessed wine, and by sharing it they ritually declare that they will now share all of their joys and sorrows, their blessings and burdens.

Amidst the scene are youths, barefoot and plainly dressed to show their status as servants.

To the left, the Apostles witness the marriage. According to the chronology of the Gospels, only five were with Him at this point, and even these had not yet received a "permanent" call—Peter, Andrew, John, Philip, and Bartholomew. Christ had yet to begin His public ministry, and He notes that His "hour is not yet come" (Jn 2:4).

But the Apostles are symbolically significant as later witnesses to the more important espousal, namely, on Holy Friday when Christ poured out His blood for His bride the Church. The Apostles were also present at the first Eucharistic miracle during the Mystical Supper.

A pious tradition states that the groom at the wedding was Simon the Zealot; his heart was pierced by the miracle and he thus decided to follow Christ. The groom here, and in most *Wedding* icons, is well-aged and round-bearded, as the Zealot typically is; however, when among the Apostles Simon is thoroughly bald, whereas the groom has a full head of hair. It is unknown to this author if the tradition associating the two is only a myth resulting from their visual similarity or if it is indeed Simon, and married life later made his hair fall out.

Amphorae

The jars used in the icon are traditional Mediterranean two-handled *amphorae*. Each presents in miniature a scene from the Old Testament. In these events God shows forth His temporal generosity, especially by miraculously feeding His people, and several of the miracles prefigure Christ and the Eucharist.

From left:
- Manna falls from heaven (Ex 16).
- Moses draws forth water from a rock (Ex 17).
- The Lord gives Israel quails to eat (Nm 11).
- Scouts return with grapes from the Promised Land, showing its fruitfulness (Nm 13:24).
- First-fruits on an altar (Ex 16).
- Elias under a juniper tree, before he received hearth cakes and water (3 Kgs 19:5).

ТОЙ ЖЕ, ХТО НАП'ЄТЬСЯ ВОДИ,
ЯКОЇ ДАМ ЙОМУ Я - НЕ МАТИМЕ
СПРАГИ ПО ВІКИ.

The Samaritan Woman at the Well

Christ, thirsty after a long journey, sits by Jacob's Well and asks a Samaritan woman to give Him a drink.

The woman, known to holy tradition as Photina, is shocked that Our Lord would speak to her, as she is both a female and a Samaritan and He is a male, a teacher, and also a Jew—and the Samaritans were schismatics in the eyes of the Jews. Christ replies, "If thou didst know the gift of God, and who he is that saith to thee, Give me to drink; thou perhaps wouldst have asked of him, and he would have given thee living water" (Jn 4:10).

She is again bewildered, for Christ has brought no implement to draw water. Our Lord replies, "Whosoever drinketh of this water, shall thirst again; but he that shall drink of the water that I will give him, shall not thirst for ever: But the water that I will give him, shall become in him a fountain of water, springing up into life everlasting" (Jn 4:13-14).

Photina is shown here gesturing for this living water.

> Jesus said to her, "Go, call thy husband, and come here." The woman answered and said, "I have no husband." Jesus said to her, "Thou hast said well, 'I have no husband,' for thou hast had five husbands: and he whom thou now hast is not thy husband. In this thou hast spoken truly" (Jn 4:16-18 *CV*).

Christ has thus proved that He miraculously knows her whole life, and the woman believes Him to be a prophet. She questions Him regarding where God wishes to be worshipped, in Jerusalem, as the Jews say, or on Samaria's Mount Gerizim. The Eternal High Priest tells her of the new hour in salvation history, when God will not be exclusively worshipped in either city, but rather "the true adorers shall adore the Father in spirit and in truth" (Jn 4:23).

She replies, "I know that the Messias cometh (who is called Christ). Therefore, when he is come, he will tell us all things" (Jn 4:25).

Jesus then declares Himself openly: "I am he, who am speaking with thee" (Jn 4:26).

To the left, the disciples, led by Peter, are surprised because their great Teacher is talking to a woman and a Samaritan. Judas, immediately behind Peter, is downright irritated. To the right, the Samaritans, hearing and believing in Our Lord, entreat Him to stay with them (Jn 4:40).

Landscape

Mount Gerizim appears behind the Samaritan crowd, for the Samaritans believed that God wished to be worshipped on that mountain, not in Jerusalem.

Feast Day:
Sunday of the Samaritan Woman - Fifth Sunday of Pascha

Troparion, Tone VIII:
At the mid-point of the Feast, O Savior, * water my thirsty soul with streams of true godliness; * for You cried out to all: "Let any who thirst, come to Me and drink." * O source of life, Christ our God, glory to You!

The city to the upper right is Sichar of Samaria, mentioned in the Gospel passage as being proximate to the event. Although most cities depicted in icons are Jerusalem, this one lacks all identifiers of being such—typically a stylized Temple or a ciborium.

Green landscapes are used in iconography to recall the Holy Spirit, Paradise, new life, and regeneration. Behind Christ and the Apostles, then, is a "spiritual meadow," taller and more lush than the brown and barren Mount Gerizim whence come the Samaritans.

Between the two groups is a form of the Jesse Tree, with a new shoot emerging from the roots.

Photina and the Well

Her name is not mentioned in the Gospel but comes rather from holy tradition; it derives from the Greek for "resplendent, shining with light." The five amphorae around the Samaritan are representative of her five husbands.

The young lady sits on Jacob's Well, depicted in the shape of a cross.

This event was foreshadowed several times in the romantic meetings of the Old Testament: when Abraham's servant found Rebecca for Isaac (Gn 24), when Jacob first saw Rachel (Gn 29:1ff.), and when Moses defended Sephora and her sisters in Madian (Ex 2:15ff.). In each case the woman became espoused to a man from the house of the chosen people. Likewise, Photina cleaves to salvation when she meets Christ at the well.

It is believed that she was eventually martyred by the Roman Emperor Nero, by being thrown down a well.

Ukrainian Inscription

ТОЙ ЖЕ, ХТО НАП'ЕТЬСЯ ВОДИ, ЯКОЇ ДАМ ЙОМУ Я~НЕ МАТИМЕ СПРАГИ ПО ВІКИ, is a paraphrase of Christ's explanation of the living water from John 4:13-14.

Christ Walking on Water

After performing the miracle of the multiplication of the loaves and fishes for five thousand men, Christ obliged the Apostles to leave by boat prior to His own exit so that He would have time to pray (Mt 14:22-23).

The boat becomes imperiled by a "contrary wind" and rough seas in the dark hours before dawn. Two Apostles cling to the rigging of the sails, which are tossed about in the blasts. The rightmost Apostle pulls at the rudder of the ship. Faces and hands convey shock and surprise, and several men cower behind their baskets.

Christ walks out on the water to meet them. A circle of serenity radiates from Him, almost a kind of "nimbus of peace" that calms the rough waves to which the rest of the water is subject.

The Apostles, taking Him for an apparition, react in fear.

But "immediately Jesus spoke to them, saying: Be of good heart: it is I, fear not. And Peter making answer, said: Lord, if it be you, bid me come to you upon the waters. And he said: Come" (Mt 14:27-29).

Yet Peter, realizing the severity of the torrent, becomes afraid and begins to sink, "And he cried out, saying: Lord, save me. And immediately Jesus stretching forth his hand took hold of him, and said to him: O you of little faith, why did you

Gospel Day:
Ninth Sunday after Pentecost

Apocalypse 14:7
Fear the Lord, and give him
honor, because the hour of
his judgment is come; and
adore ye him, that made
heaven and earth, the sea,
and the fountains of waters.

doubt" (Mt 14:30-31). Christ makes a gesture of teaching as He lovingly reaches out to grasp Peter.

Christ, Peter, and the Waters

The act of Christ walking on the sea proclaims to the Apostles that He is God, not only because it demonstrates His control over nature but also because it recalls the work of Creation described in the opening lines of Scripture: "In the beginning God created heaven, and earth. And the earth was void and empty, and darkness was upon the face of the deep; and the spirit of God moved over the waters" (Gn 1:1-2).

Christ and Peter are visibly contrasted—the hair and clothes of the latter are decidedly windswept, but Christ's are peacefully draped. The viewer thus realizes that not only the waters are calmed but the wind as well. Peter has one leg firmly planted and the other submerged, showing the imperfection of his faith. But Christ exudes complete meekness and fortitude amidst the tumult. He is our only source for peace as we struggle through the storms of life. The text, ЗАСПОКОЙТЕСЬ, ЦЕ Я, НЕ СТРАХАЙТЕСЯ!, emphasizes this fact, citing Christ's words from Matthew 14:27: "Be of good heart: it is I, fear not."

Note well that the word "meek" in modern English does not necessarily capture the idea that Christ intended when He blessed the meek during the Beatitudes (Mt 5:4). In modern English, "meek" can mean something approaching "submissive" or "weak," whereas the biblical concept is more akin to "patient," "not moved to anger," or "calm under pressure."

Although Peter is often lambasted for his weakness in this episode, the other Apostles did not even attempt to get out of the boat. Indeed, His special faith would later be recognized by Christ, who would give him "the keys of the kingdom of heaven" (Mt 16:19), that is, authority to govern His Church on earth. These keys are of course metaphorical, and Peter has not even received them at the time of this event, but the icon nevertheless has them around his neck to remind the viewer that Peter is indeed "the rock" (Mt 16:18) upon whom the faith of the Church is built.

The Apostles and the Boat

In this icon, as also in almost every icon of this series, only Peter is nimbate—the rest of the Apostles are not. This is likely an artistic decision governed by the availability of space, but it does help us to remember Peter's primacy among the Apostles.

Furthermore, the Apostles are as windswept and troubled, if not more so, than Peter is. The rightmost uselessly presses the rudder to control the boat, and the leftmost grasps his neck in terror. Others cower behind baskets, two hold on to the rigging for dear life, and one, third from the left, extends his hand in fear.

This iconographer again makes Judas obvious, the fifth from the left. His facial characteristics are consistent with depictions of Judas in the other images of the series, but apart from that he can be identified by his pinched face and because he is the only one turning his eyes from the marvel. Though he did visually witness the miracle, the icon makes clear that the eyes of his soul were willfully avoiding it.

Accompanying the Apostles are the twelve full baskets left over from the five loaves and two fishes (Mt 14:14-21). The plenitude of bread continually shared and never exhausted prefigures the Eucharistic Christ. Our Lord commands them to have charge of the fragments (Jn 6:12), and the twelve baskets indicate that these men will be the twelve patriarchs of the New Israel, which will take the Eucharist to the ends of the earth.

The Transfiguration

The text in Ukrainian, БОГ ГОСПОДЬ І ЯВИВСЯ НАМ, says, "God the Lord has appeared to us," a line taken from the Divine Liturgy for the Transfiguration and also sung by the faithful after every Eucharist.

Christ leads three of the Apostles—from left, Peter, John, and James of Zebedee—up Mount Tabor to pray, and He "was transfigured before them. And his garments became shining and exceeding white as snow" (Mk 9:1-2), white such as no earthly garment could ever be.

Christ gives the Apostles a clearer glimpse into His true resplendent glory as the uncreated Light of God. A glorious mandorla behind Him shows the breaking forth of the other world into ours and symbolizes the ineffable superabundant holiness of the God-Man.

His white and gold clothing radiates His infinite goodness, purity, perfection, and majesty.

Joining Him are Elias and Moses, "Who, appearing in glory, spoke of his death, which he was about to fulfill in Jerusalem" (Lk 9:31 *CV*).

Peter raises a hand amidst his astonished confusion and says, "Rabbi, it is good for us to be here. And let us make three tabernacles, one for you, and one for Moses, and one for Elias. For he knew not what he said: for they were struck with fear" (Mk 9:4-5).

But as Peter was speaking, "Behold a bright cloud overshadowed them. And lo a voice out of the cloud, saying: This is my beloved Son, in whom I am well pleased: hear him. And the disciples hearing fell upon their face, and were very much afraid" (Mt 17:5-6).

Peter is forced to his knees, his garment fluttering upward. He wants to see but is obliged to cover his face from the overwhelming radiance. John has fallen backwards and is trying to break his fall, and his one sandal falling off suggests the awesome force of the holiness he is witnessing. James cowers, gasping to recover his breath.

Christ, in His mercy, bids them to rise and have no fear. He points to them, ordering them to "Tell the vision to no man, till the Son of man be risen from the dead" (Mt 17:9).

The Trinity, and Knowing God

The Transfiguration was a consolation given by the Father to Christ before His Passion, and it also was intended to strengthen the Apostles for the temptations and trials they were about to endure.

All three Persons of the Trinity are made present during the Transfiguration: the voice of the Father, Christ the Son, and the "bright cloud" of the Holy Spirit, though the latter is not visible in this icon.

The Bright Cloud has several precedents in the Old Testament, including the pillar of cloud that led Moses and the Israelites (Ex 13ff.) and covered the tabernacle (Nm 9), and the cloud that filled the Temple (2 Par 5-6). It would seem at first to be a contradiction that a cloud could be "bright," but this is not so. God, and therefore the knowledge of God, is entirely beyond human understanding. His Being completely transcends being and non-being and all things (Eph 4:6), and His ways and essence are totally unsearchable (Jb 11:7-10). Therefore, knowing God does not consist in mere cogitation but in union with Him through theosis.

Christ

Christ does not undergo any fundamental change in the Transfiguration, for His glory is always present. Rather, this miracle allows the Apostles to see the glory upon which the angels have gazed from all eternity.

Similarly, in the Old Testament, a servant of the prophet Eliseus, lacking faith, worried about the multitude of Syrian armies come to assault Israel. But Eliseus prayed for his servant, saying, "Lord, open his eyes, that he may see. And the Lord opened the eyes of the servant, and he saw: and behold, the mountain was full of horses, and chariots of fire round about Eliseus" (4 Kgs 6:17). Thus, the power and glory and armies of the Lord are always around us, though unseen by our feeble physical and spiritual vision.

That humanity does not always see God and His all-surpassing glory is an unfathomable mercy upon humanity. To eyes accustomed to our dim world, the true light of the Son of God can be distressing, even unbearable. In this world it takes a special grace from God not only to witness His glory but also to endure it.

Further enhancing His luminosity are fine lines of gold paint called *assiste*. Their brightness highlights His white garment and intensifies His splendor.

Christ's supernatural glory is a visible model of theosis—that is, the human participation in the divine which is the true goal of the Catholic life. His shining form is a foretaste of the exalted bodies that will be restored to the saints at the end of time (Jn 11:24; 2 Mc 12:44) and glorified to the extent that they partook of Christ in this world (Rom 2:6; Mt 6:20).

Christ's garment and Elias' cloak indicate downward motion—they are slightly swept upward as if the subjects are arriving from above. This suggests their true heavenly home and great sanctity. Moses' robes do not appear to be swept upward in this way, but this is presumably only for artistic reasons, since he is also arriving from among the righteous departed who shall inherit heaven after Christ's resurrection.

Moses and Elias

These two figures—Moses representing the Old Law and Elias representing the prophets—bow in supplication to Christ, the One in whom the law is fulfilled and whom the prophets foretold (Mt 5:17). Their posture clearly signifies that the Old Covenant was a preparation for the New, and thus the followers of Moses and Elias should now look to Christ.

The pair also relates to Christ as a kind of "timeline" of history. On the left, Moses as a figure of the Old Law recalls the past to the viewer; Christ in the middle embodies the "eternal now" of the present; and Elias, who is thought to be one of the "two witnesses" who will come at the end of the world (Apoc 11:3), signifies the future. Here, beyond of all mortal understanding, the past and the future talk with the present, a glimpse of that eternal conversation outside of time. Together the three are a synopsis of the whole of salvation history, known by God before the beginning of the World.

Their posture further recalls a *deisis* representation of Christ. A deisis usually shows Him in majesty, and bowing to Him are Mary and John the Forerunner on either side, sometimes accompanied by other saints.

Perched upon Elias' shoulder is a raven with a morsel in his beak, one of those that brought the prophet "bread and flesh" (3 Kgs 17:6) when he was hiding from the wicked King Achab of Israel; this sustenance miraculously brought to Elias prefigures the miraculous spiritual sustenance we receive in the Eucharist. Fire leaps about his feet in reference to the fire of the Lord that he witnessed (3 Kgs 18:38) and to the chariot of fire that carried him from this life (4 Kgs 2:11) and is a manifestation that recalls the blazing light of Christ's divinity that is visible during the Transfiguration.

Moses is a young man in this icon, unlike the elder, more patriarchal Moses of our iconostasis. He wears royal purple. His scroll reads, "If the Lord be God, follow him" (3 Kgs 18:21). The lawgiver holds stone tablets containing the Decalogue—the Ten Commandments. The language is Hebrew, and is read right-to-left: יהוה, that is, YHWH, the Sacred Name of God, also called the *Tetragrammaton*.

Moses and Elias discuss the trials to come, teaching us that our glory is only attained through the cross. They saw God indirectly—the Burning Bush, the pillar of fire, the light on Mount Sinai, the fire on Mount Carmel, and the chariot of fire. But on Mount Tabor, God's radiance is seen directly.

Apostles

Transfiguration has a strongly hierarchical composition: the glorified and perfect Christ, the God-Man, is highest; below Him are the human yet heavenly and exalted Elias and Moses; and at the bottom are the lowly Apostles, still working out their salvation on earth.

It is instructive to compare the confusion and tumult of the Apostles in *Transfiguration* with their sublime investure with power and authority in *Descent of the Holy Spirit*. In the former they are overwhelmed by the manifestation of God's glory, but in the latter God gives them the grace to confront Him with peace and confidence.

Iconodulia

The Transfiguration demonstrates that the power of God can shine forth through His material creation. Now that God has taken on human flesh, the material world, which is of its nature good but fallen, has been remade. Matter may mediate the grace of God, not through its inherent qualities (such as with a "magical" talisman or amulet) but because the Lord freely allows it to do so.

This is an important concept to know in order to understand *iconodulia*, that is, the veneration of icons. Icons are not themselves Christ's body, but neither are His garments during the Transfiguration, and these garments certainly transmitted the splendor of His divine power. Thus, other matter—including icons and relics—can communicate the sacred and be a source of grace to the pious believer.

An important distinction should here be made between the two or three types of "worship" in the Catholic Church. The most basic is called *dulia*, which means approximately "veneration." It is that honor paid to the saints or to icons, relics, and sacred places. In such cases, the person or thing *in itself* is not worthy of veneration; rather, it points to something greater than itself, and the veneration paid to it is passed on to the original, or *archetype*.

Dulia is similar to human honor paid to important people or things. When a reasonable person salutes a flag or kisses a picture of a departed loved one, he is not expressing his love for the mere items; rather, he is honoring the nation or person called to mind.

This differs from *latria*, which is true adoration due to God alone and given to Him for His own sake.

As an example, when we venerate an icon of St. Peter, we honor the icon because it is an image of Peter whom we love, and we honor Peter as far as he is a reflection of Christ our God, whom we adore. Both the icon and Peter are only means—beloved and special, but still only means—whereas the blessed and glorious Trinity is the end.

A special subtype of dulia exists called *hyperdulia*, which is a greater veneration reserved for the Mother of God as the most perfect partaker of the divine nature. It is finite like regular dulia, and still it is due to Mary only because she leads us to the infinite latria due to God alone.

All three of these words have historically been translated into English as "worship," and indeed it is accurate to do so. But because after the Protestant iconoclasm many confuse the types of worship, it is now preferable to use the more precise words "veneration" and "adoration."

The Raising of Lazarus

Martha, sister of the recently deceased Lazarus—both friends of Our Lord—cries to Him that if He had been present, He could have preserved the life of her brother. And Jesus says to her,

> "Thy brother shall rise." Martha said to him, "I know that he shall rise again, in the resurrection at the last day." Jesus said to her, "I am the resurrection and the life: he that believes in me, even if he die, shall live; and whoever lives and believes in me, shall never die. Dost thou believe this?" She said to him, "Yes, Lord, I believe that thou art the Christ, the Son of God, who hast come into the world" (Jn 11:23-27 *CV*).

Jesus then sends Martha to fetch her sister Mary, who also bewails the fact that He could have saved Lazarus' life. Christ, now present at the tomb, weeps for His friend (Jn 11:35). Seeing the sisters' sorrow and hearing certain Jews (not pictured) contemptuously question why He could heal a blind man but not save Lazarus (Jn 11:37), Jesus commands them to roll away the stone of the tomb.

Martha, on her knees but upright, lower center, protests that her brother has been dead for four days, such that his corpse will already have a foul smell. Two men assisting at the tomb, center, testify to this reality, covering their faces to repel the stench, their eyes betraying distaste for the deathly aroma.

But Christ reminds her that those who believe will see the glory of God, and making a motion of command, "He cried with a loud voice: Lazarus, come forth. And presently he that had been dead came forth, bound feet and hands with winding bands" (Jn 11:43-44).

The Apostles, left—wide-eyed and jaws agape—look at each other in astonishment at Christ's victory over Lazarus' death.

Many of the Jews, having witnessed this prodigy, believed in Him, but some reported Him to the Pharisees, who from "that day…devised to put him to death" (Jn 11:53). Thus the raising of Lazarus set in motion the evil deeds that culminated in Christ's Passion and Resurrection.

Feast Day:
Lazarus Saturday -
Sixth Saturday of the Great Fast

Troparion, Tone I:
Assuring us before Your Passion
of the general resurrection, *
You raised Lazarus from the
dead, O Christ God; * and so,
like the children, we also carry
signs of victory * and cry to
You, the conqueror of death:
* Hosanna in the highest! *
Blessed is He who comes *
in the name of the Lord.

Christ and Lazarus

Christ's tears reveal His true human emotions—reminding us that God the Son is truly man, like us in all things but sin.

Lazarus was dead for four days and as such prefigures Christ's three days in the tomb. This miracle also gives hope and encouragement to His followers as the time of His Passion approaches. Lazarus wears a burial shroud that is reminiscent of swaddling clothes and thus connects death with new life. He proceeds from the black cave of his tomb, calling to mind the conquest of death and visually paralleling the escape of the righteous from Hades in *Anastasis*.

Lazarus' resurrection is also a foretaste of the general resurrection, when the souls of all of the faithful will be reunited with their bodies.

Mary and Martha

Mary has in front of her a jar of ointment that she will later use to anoint Christ's feet (Jn 12:1-8), one of which she touches with her robed hand. Mary is several times depicted in the Gospels as the holier of the two, because of her deeper faith prior to her brother's resurrection and because she listened attentively to Christ while Martha busied herself with hospitality toward her guests (Lk 10:38-42). Jesus tells Martha that the contemplative Mary "hath chosen the best part" (Lk 10:42).

Mary's greater spiritual progress is reflected in her bow of deepest reverence, a *proskynesis*, a sign of her complete trust in and submission to the Author of Life. Still, the devoted Martha also kneels and covers her hands.

The Ukrainian inscription, Я ВОСКРЕСІННЯ І ЖИТТЯ, is the central message of Christ's conversation with Martha: "I am the Resurrection and the Life."

Tomb Assistants

These two men wince and gag as they confront the reeking tomb. In doing so they testify that Lazarus was truly dead, and thus Christ has power over life and death.

Their hands are covered not as a sign of reverence but because they are defending themselves from the fetid stench.

Another man sets down the heavy stone lid of the crypt, a detail not mentioned in Scripture. This recalls the rolling away of the stone from Christ's tomb. The crypt also echoes the manger in *Nativity*, another connection between death and new life.

A willow bush hints at Christ's approaching triumphal procession into Jerusalem, when He will be briefly and imperfectly proclaimed as the conquering prince that He is.

Simultaneous Narration

Raising of Lazarus makes extensive use of simultaneous narration. The sisters arrive, Christ orders, the tomb is opened, Lazarus arises, and all the spectators react, all seemingly at the same time. But most notably, an entirely separate episode is tucked away in the background.

Second Scene: Man Born Blind at the Pool of Siloam

This event occurred prior to the raising of Lazarus, and it was mentioned by some of those who scoffed at Christ's apparent inability to prevent Lazarus' death (Jn 11:37). Christ came upon a man blind from birth. The disciples, adhering to the then-common belief that such misfortunes were the direct result of sin, questioned Him:

> "Rabbi, who has sinned, this man or his parents, that he should be born blind?" Jesus answered, "Neither has this man sinned, nor his parents, but the works of God were to be made manifest in him. I must work the works of him who sent me while it is day; night is coming, when no one can work. As long as I am in the world I am the light of the world (Jn 9:2-5 *CV*).

In performing this miracle, Our Lord ordered the blind man to wash in the Pool of Siloam, the so-named city visible in the background. Above the pool is a tower with an obvious crack, representing the structure in Siloam that fell and killed eighteen men (Lk 13:4). The tower is included here as visual shorthand to show that this mini-scene takes place in Siloam rather than in the same location as the central events of the icon. Christ cited the example of the fallen tower when explaining that bad things can happen to good people.

Feast Day:
Sunday of the Man Born Blind
- Sixth Sunday of Pascha

Kontakion, Tone IV:
Blinded in the eyes of my soul,
* I come to You, O Christ, like
the man who was blind from
birth, * and I cry in repentance:
* You are the brilliant light
of those in darkness.

The Question of the Rich Young Man

A wealthy youth kneels before Christ and asks Him what he must do to attain everlasting life (Mt 19:16).

Christ bids him to keep the commandments, but the man insists that he has always done this—what else must he do? Our Lord motions with an open hand to the beggars, upper right, and replies, "If you will be perfect, go sell what you have, and give to the poor, and you shall have treasure in heaven: and come, follow me" (Mt 19:21-22). But the young man, having a great many possessions, left disheartened. Our Teacher makes use of this moment, saying, "Amen, I say to you, that a rich man shall hardly enter into the kingdom of heaven. And again I say to you: It is easier for a camel to pass through the eye of a needle, than for a rich man to enter into the kingdom of heaven" (Mt 19:23-24).

The Apostles, especially Peter, express their dismay, wondering who could possibly be saved under such incredible standards.

Yet Our Lord reassures them, not in themselves, but in the grace of God: "With men this is impossible: but with God all things are possible" (Mt 19:26).

Christ

Our Lord sits in front of a typical depiction of the Temple of Jerusalem, making a gesture of teaching. He is seated to emphasize His authority, as this was the posture of religious and secular educators in antiquity. Unlike today, in ancient times the more important person was allowed to relax at leisure, and students were typically required to stand as a sign of respect.

The text, РОЗДАЙ БІДНИМ І БУДЕШ МАТИ СКАРБ НА НЕБІ!, is Christ's great lesson in this passage: "Give to the poor, and you shall have treasure in heaven."

Rich Man and Beggars

The youth is earnest, reverent, and well-intentioned, though perhaps not yet able to accept the challenge of perfection offered by Our Lord. Actual material poverty is not required of every Christian, though poverty of spirit is; unfortunately, the young man demonstrates that he lacks them both.

His sparse incipient beard displays his young age.

The young man is clothed in splendid wealthy attire—the expensive colors purple and blue; jewels on his cloak, clasp, socks, and buskins; ostentatious rings; an embroidered and jeweled chiton; finely styled hair in the Late Antique style; and a hefty purse hanging from a chain. He also kneels on a pillow commonly used by the wealthy.

Gospel Day:
Twelfth Sunday after Pentecost

Apocalypse 3:17-18
Because thou sayest: I am rich, and made wealthy, and have need of nothing: and knowest not, that thou art wretched, and miserable, and poor, and blind, and naked. * I counsel thee to buy of me gold fire tried, that thou mayest be made rich; and mayest be clothed in white garments, and that the shame of thy nakedness may not appear; and anoint thy eyes with eyesalve, that thou mayest see.

Psalm 118:173-176
Let thy hand be with me to
save me; for I have chosen thy
precepts. * I have longed for
thy salvation, O Lord; and thy
law is my meditation. * My
soul shall live and shall praise
thee: and thy judgments shall
help me. * I have gone astray
like a sheep that is lost: seek
thy servant, because I have not
forgotten thy commandments.

The rich man's posture mirrors that of the nearest poor man, save for the closed arms of the youth. One wears sumptuous apparel, and the other tatters. One has a beautiful curly coiffure, the other a haggard beard and head of hair. One kneels on a brocade rug, the other on bare ground. One carries a fat purse, the other an empty beggar's bowl. One wears a face of contentment, the other of extreme distress.

The former asks for wisdom, but the latter does not have that luxury, and begs only for sustenance.

The other beggars are in a condition similar to that of the first.

Perfection

The Church does not take Christ's words about perfection to mean that all of His followers must repeatedly give away all of their belongings in order to be saved. Voluntary poverty along with chastity and obedience are considered to be Christ's *evangelical counsels*—in other words, they are His recommendation as to the surest path to holiness and salvation, but they are not binding on all Catholics.

Those that live *consecrated lives* publicly profess—usually before a Church authority in a solemn ceremony—to follow these counsels. These heroes compose the various ranks of lay and clerical life, from consecrated virgins and widows living in the secular world on up through members of the clergy and of religious orders.

The Calling of Zacheus

Our Lord enters Jericho, where a great crowd congregates around Him.

One publican named Zacheus, being a short man, is unable to see Christ and climbs a sycamore tree to get a better view. Our Lord approaches him, looks gently upon him, motions in a teaching manner, and says, "Zacheus, make haste and come down; for this day I must abide in thy house" (Lk 19:5). Christ seems to offer His scroll of divine Wisdom to the seeker.

Zacheus promptly came down and "received him with joy" (Lk 19:6).

Many among the crowd express vexation because Christ, a Jew and a reputable rabbi, has deigned to consort with a publican—one that collects taxes for the hated Roman conquerors, and perhaps dishonestly at that. Peter, visible behind Christ, touches his hand to his chest and gestures as if to say, "Slow down there, what are you doing?"

But Zacheus humbles himself before the Lord, remarking that he will now give half of his goods to the poor, and will restore fourfold to any person he has wronged.

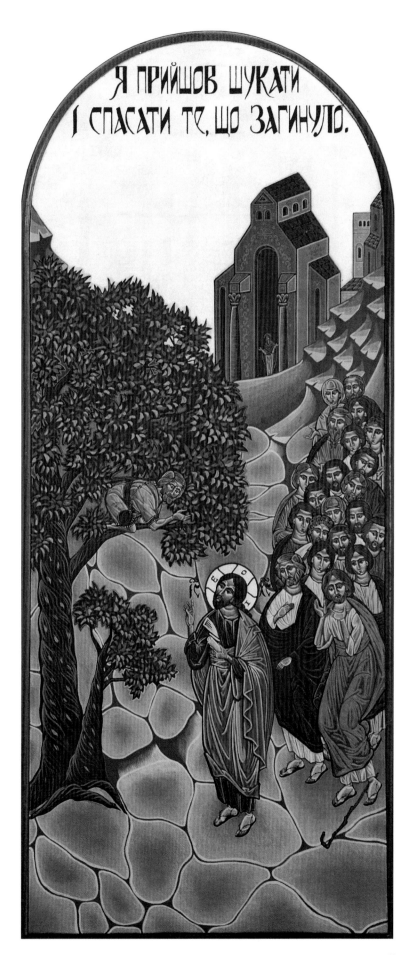

Я ПРИЙШОВ ШУКАТИ
І СПАСАТИ ТЕ, ЩО ЗАГИНУЛО.

And so "Jesus said to him: This day is salvation come to this house, because he also is a son of Abraham. For the Son of man is come to seek and to save that which was lost" (Lk 19:9-10).

Christ and Zacheus

The Savior and His newest disciple converse within the city of Jericho.

The publican's name in the original Hebrew means "pure and righteous one." He, although up in a tree, is clearly in a posture of worship, and his hand indicates that he is speaking to Christ. Although Zacheus' reply took place when he was on the ground, the icon here uses simultaneous narration to express multiple events in the same scene.

The smaller sapling springing up from the roots of the tree is another allusion to Christ as the "rod out of the root of Jesse" (Is 11:1).

Zacheus' wealth is shown by his blue and purple colors, his jeweled and embroidered garments, and the large money pouch hanging from his upper body.

Holy tradition believes that he followed Peter, who eventually appointed him bishop of Caesarea in Palestine, and that he died peacefully.

Both he and the rich young man are wealthy, both are Jews, and both are in some sense living righteous lives; yet worldly things are an obstacle for the respectable youth, who is reluctant to abandon his life to Christ. These two icons together teach us that the esteem of society, while neither inherently good nor bad, can be a serious impediment to a life of devotion and sanctity.

At that time, the fruit of the sycamore tree was fed to pigs, and therefore it was generally avoided by Jews. Zacheus willingly took upon himself this humiliation in pursuit of God, and for this sacrifice he was richly rewarded by his Master—his name, scorned by his acquaintances during his fleeting years on earth, is now perpetually remembered and celebrated by the faithful for all time.

Ukrainian Inscription

Я ПРИЙШОВ ШУКАТИ І СПАСАТИ ТЕ, ЩО ЗАГИНУЛО are Christ's words here, but spoken in the first person: "I came to seek and to save that which was lost."

Second Scene: Blind Man on the Road to Jericho

Gospel Day:
Thirty-First Sunday
after Pentecost

Psalm 145:8-10
The Lord enlighteneth the
blind. The Lord lifteth up
them that are cast down: the
Lord loveth the just. * The
Lord keepeth the strangers,
he will support the fatherless
and the widow: and the ways
of sinners he will destroy.
* The Lord shall reign for
ever: thy God, O Sion, unto
generation and generation.

Immediately before He arrived in the city, Christ passed by a blind man who, upon hearing that the great miracle worker was approaching, exclaimed, "Jesus, son of David, have mercy on me" (Lk 18:38). The crowd attempted to shush him, but he cried out all the more: "Son of David, have mercy on me" (Lk 18:39).

Taking notice, Christ asks him what he wants, and he replies with eloquent simplicity, "Lord, that I may see" (Lk 18:41). Jesus readily grants his request: "Receive thy sight: thy faith hath made thee whole" (Lk 18:42). Immediately the man was able to see; he gave glory to God and followed Our Lord.

To the lower right, simultaneous narration is again used: the formerly blind man, wide-eyed with shock and looking at his hands, has dropped his now unneeded cane and is at the front of the crowd walking after Our Lord.

This little additional scene further reinforces how blessed are those who do not allow fear of small-minded public opinion to squelch their thirst for God.

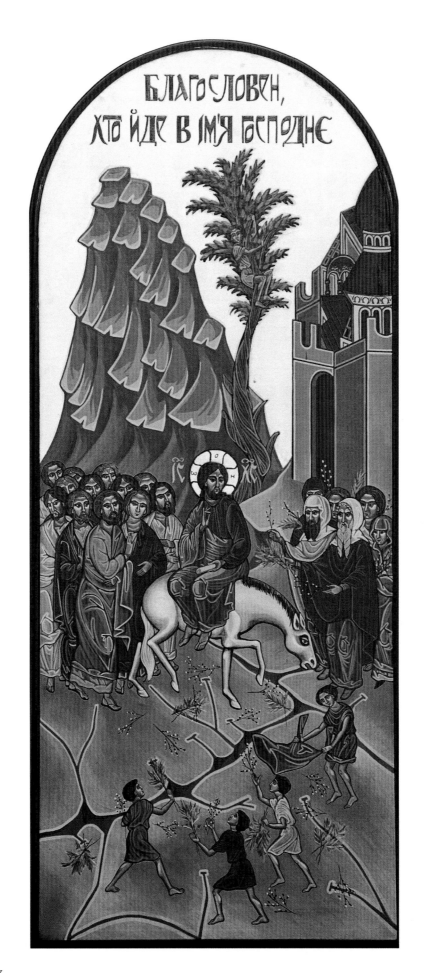

The Entrance into Jerusalem

Our Lord rides a colt from Mount Olivet, left, followed by the Twelve Apostles and cheered by the populace, who wave palm and willow branches to welcome the conquering King, crying, "Hosanna to the son of David: Blessed is he that cometh in the name of the Lord: Hosanna in the highest" (Mt 21:9).

Foreknowing the destruction of Jerusalem, and in His mercy lamenting what is hidden from the eyes of the now joyful inhabitants, Christ looks out sorrowfully over the crowd. As He approaches the city, He weeps for it, saying to Jerusalem,

> For days will come upon thee when thy enemies will throw up a rampart about thee, and surround thee and shut thee in on every side, and will dash thee to the ground and thy children within thee, and will not leave in thee one stone upon another, because thou hast not known the time of thy visitation (Lk 19:43-44 CV).

A youth climbs a palm tree to cut down additional fronds.

Another youth spreads out a tunic underneath Him, at that time an act of homage performed by children to welcome the appointment of a new king.

Judas, far left, scowls, his pride alienating him from the spiritual glory before him. Sharing in his attitude are the chief priests of the Temple and the scribes, not pictured, who as the current leaders of the people express contempt for Him whom they consider a usurper.

Inconsistent Perspective

In this icon, Jerusalem is depicted with a strongly *inconsistent perspective*: walls and buildings are not to appropriate scale and are painted with impossible geometry, and lines of sight clash. This technique is common in iconography to indicate otherworldliness, but when done to this degree, it communicates that the object displayed has a singularly symbolic nature in the depiction.

In this case, Jerusalem represents the Church that Christ establishes, every soul that receives Him, and, ultimately, the kingdom of heaven, which He will soon open to mankind through His glorious conquest of death and Hades.

Christ

Palm Sunday fulfills the prophecy of Zacharias: "Rejoice greatly, O daughter of Sion, shout for joy, O daughter of Jerusalem: BEHOLD THY KING will come to thee, the just and saviour: he is poor, and riding upon an ass, and upon a colt the foal of an ass" (Zac 9:9).

Feast Day:
Palm / Willow / Green Sunday - Sixth Sunday of the Great Fast

Kontakion, Tone VI:
Mounted on the throne in heaven, O Christ God, * and on a colt here on earth, * You accepted the praise of the angels, * and the hymn of the children who cried to You: * Bless'd are You, Who have come to call Adam back.

This event recalls the custom of the ancient world in which a triumphal conqueror rode into a city. *Entrance* borrows from the popular Imperial Roman *adventus* art motif, which depicts an emperor formally arriving through the gates of a city followed by a long train of soldiers, numerous attendants, and a joyous throng of locals. But instead of a mighty steed of conquest, Christ rides a humble colt; and instead of a parade of proud warriors, He is followed by the uncertain and misunderstanding Apostles.

Christ our King is not situated such as one would naturally ride on an animal, but rather He sits as on a throne, emphasizing His royalty.

The Son of God is not here actively exercising His kingly power and authority, nor does He demand at sword point that His arrival be celebrated; yet the people, recalling His astonishing miracles and profound doctrines, recognize Him as their sovereign and glorify Him. Christ our Teacher leads by example, entering the city with the humility that we also should practice. His authority as divine Teacher is also conveyed by His act of sitting while His spiritual pupils stand, and He holds His hand in a didactic posture.

Crowds and Children

For the only time in His earthly life, Christ is proclaimed as the Son of David, the Messiah.

The text, БЛАГОСЛОВЕН ХТО ЙДЕ В ІМ'Я ГОСПОДНЕ, is the acclamation of the crowd: "Blessed is He who comes in the name of the Lord."

Palms are a symbol of victory from Antique Mediterranean culture, but because the Slavic peoples had no access to palms for the celebration of this day, willow branches were substituted. This custom is recalled in the icon, even though willows were not used during the actual event.

There is no explicit mention of children in the Gospels, though Matthew does say that "a very great multitude spread their garments in the way: and others cut boughs from the trees, and strewed them in the way" (Mt 21:8); one may safely presume that children are present wherever there is a "very great multitude."

But the young play a more important role here: they symbolize those spiritual children that look upon Christ with fresh and innocent eyes, devoid of any corrupt or selfish motivations. They stand in contrast to others who expect the Savior to be a conquering hero like Simon Machabeus (1 Mc 13-16, esp. 13:51), slaughtering his enemies and bestowing worldly prosperity upon Israel. Against them King David testifies, "Out of the mouth of infants and of sucklings thou hast perfected praise" (Ps 8:3), and Christ said, "Amen I say to you, whosoever shall not receive the kingdom of God as a little child shall not enter into it" (Mk 10:15).

Judas

Judas' face shows that by the time of the Entrance his will is hardened against Christ, and he is on the verge of betraying the Master.

Just prior to the Entrance, Mary, the sister of Lazarus, used a pound of expensive spikenard perfume to anoint Our Lord. Judas questioned her action, asking why the pricey commodity was not instead sold and the proceeds given to the poor. The Gospel of John notes that Judas had no concern for the poor; rather, he said this only because he handled the finances, and being a thief he would steal from the purse (Jn 12:6).

Christ rebuked him, saying, "Let her alone, that she may keep it against the day of my burial. For the poor you have always with you; but me you have not always" (Jn 12:7-8). And to emphasize the virtue of Mary's action, He declares, "Amen, I say to you, wheresoever this gospel shall be preached in the whole world, that also which she hath done, shall be told for a memorial of her" (Mk 14:9).

And so in his indignation Judas thereafter went to the chief priests to betray Christ. His sour, pouting face reminds the viewer that Christ is going to Jerusalem not to reign as a worldly king but to die as a victim for sinners.

The Complaint of Judas and Sacred Art

This incident is of further import. Our Lord here makes plain that reverencing Him, the Creator and Ruler of the universe, is an obligation prior to our own welfare and even that of our fellow man. Thus, the honor the Church gives to God through the expense of its sacred art, architecture, incense, and music are right and proper because God deserves them. Indeed, the testimony of centuries of Catholic civilization teaches us that the greatest of sacred monuments were built with voluntary gifts of money and labor from poor people—those same who would have benefited from Judas' disordered notion of charity.

Joining their voices to that of the betrayer, many modern critics care little for the poor, but they nevertheless find the expense of art and liturgy to be a convenient stick with which to beat Holy Mother Church.

The Great Entrance

The Entrance into Jerusalem is re-presented to us every Sunday during the Divine Liturgy when the priest carries bread and wine from the prothesis table at liturgical north, out through St. Michael's door, and back in through the Royal Doors.

The Eucharistic elements are thereby brought to the sacrifice in a manner that reminds us of how Our Lord carried His own sacred body and blood into Jerusalem for His consummate and eternal sacrifice. This portion of the liturgy is therefore called *The Great Entrance*.

РЕВНІСТЬ ДОМУ ТВОГО ПОЇДАТИМЕ МЕНЕ!

Christ Cleanses the Temple

Our Lord, angered by the commerce and exploitation occurring in the Temple, fashions a "scourge of little cords" (Jn 2:15) and drives out the money changers, overturning their tables and spilling their coinage. His blue himation shows rapid movement, and He makes a pushing gesture with one hand and swings the whip with the other.

Christ also chases away the merchants of sacrificial livestock. An ox rears up from the scourge, two lambs look back as they run away, and two doves take flight.

The furious vendors, right, cower and flee the scene.

Our Lord then explains, "Is it not written, My house shall be called the house of prayer to all nations? But you have made it a den of thieves" (Mk 11:17). And "to them that sold doves he said: Take these things hence, and make not the house of my Father a house of traffic" (Jn 2:16).

Seeing the commotion, Christ's disciples remember Psalm 68:10: "The zeal of thy house hath eaten me up." The Apostles, left, gaze in astonishment as Christ defends His Father's honor and asserts His teachings. They also represent the joyful crowds who watched in wonder and praised Our Lord with hosannas.

The chief priests and scribes of the Temple show consternation, and "they sought how they might destroy him. For they feared him, because the whole multitude was in admiration at his doctrine" (Mt 11:18).

Antiphon III:
Response: Christ is risen from the dead, * trampling death by death, * and to those in the tombs giving life.

Let God arise, and let his enemies be scattered: and let them that hate him flee from before his face (Ps 67:2). (*Response*) * As smoke vanisheth, so let them vanish away: as wax melteth before the fire (Ps 67:3). (*Response*) * So let the wicked perish at the presence of God. And let the just feast, and rejoice before God: and be delighted with gladness (Ps 67:3-4). (*Response*)

Court of the Gentiles

A prayer shawl, hanging over steps and tied to a ciborium and a column, alerts the viewer that this takes place inside the confines of the Temple; specifically, in the Court of the Gentiles, where non-Jewish believers in the God of Israel could go and pray to Him. Over time, the court came to be used to exchange goods needed in the Temple rituals and to convert the monies of diverse lands into currency accepted by the Temple.

Sacrificial Animals

Oxen are mentioned repeatedly in Numbers 7 as part of "sacrifices of peace offerings" before God.

Lambs began as sacrificial animals during Israel's time in Egypt, when Moses commanded them to go and "take a lamb by your families, and sacrifice the Phase. And dip a bunch of hyssop in the blood that is at the door, and sprinkle the transom of the door therewith, and both the door cheeks" (Ex 12:21-22). The angel who was to slay the firstborn of Egypt would then pass by the houses so marked. Thereafter, the sacrifice of lambs was regularized into Israel's worship as a way to beg God for peace and the remission of sin.

This ritual is an obvious prefigurement of the blood of the Lamb of God, which has been shed for us and for all to bring remission of sins and peace between man and his Creator.

Turtle doves or pigeons were a sacrifice offered under the Old Law by those unable to afford more expensive livestock. Saint Joseph, the foster-father of Our Lord, was among these poor, for such did he offer during the Presentation of Our Lord.

That Christ the Lamb of God drove out these fauna foreshadows that He will soon replace them as the one sacrifice acceptable to the Eternal Father.

The New Israel

When Christ overturns the tables, He says to those around, "My house shall be called the house of prayer; but you have made it a den of thieves" (Mt 21:13). In so doing he references Isaias, where he prophesied God's eventual conversion of the Gentiles:

> And the children of the stranger that adhere to the Lord, to worship him, and to love his name, to be his servants: every one that keepeth the sabbath from profaning it, and that holdeth fast my covenant: I will bring them into my holy mount, and will make them joyful in my house of prayer: their holocausts, and their victims shall please me upon my altar: for my house shall be called the house of prayer, for all nations (Is 56:6-7).

Christ also draws from Jeremias, who told Israel that they could not continue "to steal, to murder, to commit adultery, to swear falsely, to offer to Baalim, and to go after strange gods" (Jer 7:9) and then presume that mere adherence to the Temple service would save them. The Lord, through Jeremias, asks rhetorically, "Is this house then, in which my name hath been called upon, in your eyes become a den of robbers?" (Jer 7:11)—that is, they cannot hide behind the Temple while neglecting true repentance.

And so in referencing these passages while disrupting the sacrifices of the Old Law, the Just One prophesies that the Temple will soon cease to function as man's connection to God. Indeed, it would be utterly destroyed in AD 70 by the future Roman emperor Titus, never again to see the sacrifices of the Old Covenant. He further makes known that the New Israel, the Church, will be drawn from all nations.

Unfortunately, not all the children of Israel will accept the change; these obstinate ones are represented by the central scribe, who clings tightly to his Torah scroll and looks directly at the viewer in defiance.

Ukrainian Inscription

РЕВНІСТЬ ДОМУ ТВОГО ПОЇДАТИМЕ МЕНЕ translates to a slightly different rendering of Psalm 68:10: "Zeal of thy house shall devour me."

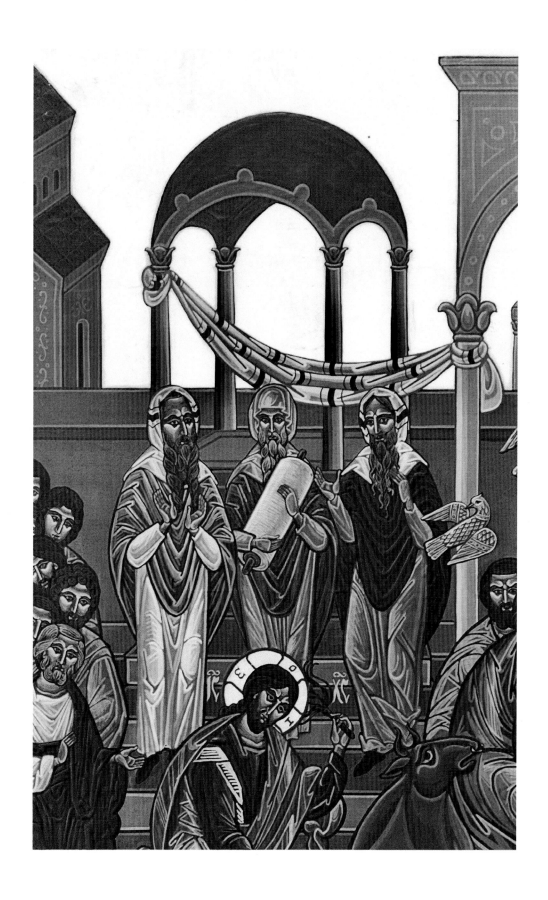

Feast Day:
Great and Holy Thursday

Troparion, Tone VIII (*HT*):
When Thy glorious Disciples
were enlightened at the supper
by the feet washing, * then the
impious Judas was darkened
with the disease of avarice, *
and he delivered Thee, the Just
Judge, to the lawless judges. *
See, O lover of money, * this
man through money came
to hang himself. * Flee the
insatiable desire which dared to
do such things to the Master.
* O Lord, Who art good
towards all, glory to Thee.

Я ХЛІБ ЖИТТЯ,
ЯКИЙ З НЕБА ЗІЙШОВ

The Mystical Supper

While celebrating the Pascha of the Old Law, Christ looks directly at the viewer and blesses the bread and wine upon the table. He thus presents His death to His Apostles and to us, teaching us how we will worship Him under the New Law: "This is my body, which is given for you. Do this for a commemoration of me" (Lk 22:19).

But as Paul later notes,

> For as often as you shall eat this bread, and drink the chalice, you shall shew the death of the Lord, until he come. Therefore whosoever shall eat this bread, or drink the chalice of the Lord unworthily, shall be guilty of the body and of the blood of the Lord. But let a man prove himself: and so let him eat of that bread, and drink of the chalice (1 Cor 11:26-28).

Judas, again notably lacking a nimbus, impertinently grasps his morsel, signifying that he is the betrayer. And thus we are reminded that even from the beginning some approached the Eucharist unworthily.

John, in contrast, leans devotedly upon the bosom of Our Lord.

Peter puts his hand to his chest in surprise, and all the other Apostles—evidently still oblivious to His wondrous doctrine—converse regarding who will betray Him (Mt 26:21-22) and "which of them should seem to be the greater" (Lk 22:24) and therefore of higher authority.

The upper portions and peaks of buildings are visible, indicating that the icon takes place upstairs, in the "upper room" mentioned in some translations of Mark 14:15.

Christ, John, and Judas

Christ and John look directly at us.

The icon draws a clear distinction between the prideful Judas, with his squinted and mistrusting eyes looking directly up at Christ, snatching his portion, and the beloved John, whose face is cast down like the humble publican (Lk 18:13) and whose arms are folded in the manner of a worshipper approaching the Eucharist.

Bread and Wine

In Ukrainian are Christ's words that succinctly capture the essence of the Eucharistic Mystery: Я ХЛІБ ЖИТТЯ, ЯКИЙ З НЕБА ЗІЙШОВ—"I am the bread of life" (Jn 6:35).

The Eucharistic elements of bread and wine are displayed prominently in this image. There are twelve loaves here, eleven of which are still laid out on the table, a clear reference to the Loaves of Proposition in the Old Law (Ex 25; Lv 24).

Those twelve loaves are accompanied by seven vessels of wine; together the bread and wine teach us that the Eucharist will be given to both the Twelve Tribes of Israel and the Gentiles, who are represented by the seven nations that the Lord ordered destroyed out of the Promised Land (Dt 7:1). Seven and twelve also echo the two multiplications of loaves and fishes—in one instance twelve baskets of fragments were filled (Jn 6:13) and in the other seven were filled (Mt 15:37).

The Crucifixion

After He was shamelessly betrayed by Judas and mercilessly abused by Jews and Romans alike, Our Lord was led to Golgotha: "They crucified him, and with him two others, one on each side, and Jesus in the midst" (Jn 19:18).

This icon makes extensive use of simultaneous narration. The many events depicted here actually happened one after another, but they are portrayed together so as to condense a great deal of meaning into one image.

An inscription board above Our Lord, known as the *titulus crucis*, states "in letters of Greek, and Latin, and Hebrew: THIS IS THE KING OF THE JEWS" (Lk 23:38).

Our Lady weeps, her hand raised in sorrow. Mary Magdalene and Mary of Cleopas attempt to console her (Jn 19:25). Magdalene's unkempt hair has escaped from her maphorion, demonstrating that she has lost herself in emotion.

The beloved disciple John the Theologian laments over the death of Christ, his hand to his cheek.

The Redeemer gives Our Lady to John and all Christians: "He saith to his mother: Woman, behold thy son. After that, he saith to the disciple: Behold thy mother. And from that hour, the disciple took her to his own" (Jn 19:26-27)—as should we.

The bad thief, to our right, wears a surly expression, blaspheming Our Lord and insisting that if He is indeed Christ then He should save them all. But the penitent thief, nimbate, rebuked him, saying:

> Neither dost thou fear God, seeing thou art condemned under the same condemnation? And we indeed justly, for we receive the due reward of our deeds; but this man hath done no evil. And he said to Jesus: Lord, remember me when thou shalt come into thy kingdom. And Jesus said to him: Amen I say to thee, this day thou shalt be with me in paradise (Lk 23:40-43).

Christ, toward the end of His Passion, declared that He was thirsty. To our right, a man, his face broadcasting his ill intent, with "a sponge full of vinegar and hyssop, put it to his mouth. Jesus therefore, when he had taken the vinegar, said: It is consummated. And bowing his head, he gave up the ghost" (Jn 19:29-30).

Christ's fallen countenance and single lock of hair out of place show us that He has expired.

As Christ dies, a great earthquake tears through the rocks, here leaving a black opening. Also, though not portrayed here, the veil of the Temple is rent in two, and many of the righteous departed returned to life and came into Jerusalem (Mt 27:51-53). To right, "The centurion and they that were with him watching

Feast Day:
Great and Holy Friday

Aposticha, Tone V:
You were naked and cold in death, * O You Who wear light as a robe, * and the noble Joseph and Nicodemus * removed You from the Cross, * with grief and tears so tender. * And Joseph mourned and prayed: * O what has happened, O gentle Jesus? * The sun saw You suspended on the Cross * and shrouded itself in darkness. * The earth quaked with fear * and the temple veil was rent asunder! * For my sake, O Savior, You willingly endured the Passion. * How then shall I array Your Body, O my God? * How then shall I wrap You in this shroud? * How then shall I hymn Your burial? * O my Lord most merciful, * Your death and rising shall I praise * as I sing: O Lord, glory be to You!

Jesus, having seen the earthquake, and the things that were done, were sore afraid, saying: Indeed this was the Son of God" (Mt 27:54).

To ensure that Christ was dead, "One of the soldiers with a spear opened his side, and immediately there came out blood and water" (Jn 19:34), signifying, among other things, the saving mysteries of the Eucharist and baptism, respectively.

Christ and the Thieves

Above the scene is the Ukrainian inscription ВОЗНІССЯ ТИ НА ХРЕСТ ВОЛЕЮ СВОЕЮ: "You ascended the cross by Your will," a slightly different translation of the opening of the kontak of the Exaltation of the Holy Cross.

The Savior's garment is red, vividly recalling His sacrifice in blood. It also reminds us that this is the moment of His glorious victory—He is the Savior who tramples His enemies, His apparel stained with their blood (Is 63:2-4).

The Ukrainian on the titulus translates as "Glorious King."

The repentant thief is not named in Holy Scripture, but according to the apocryphal *Gospel of Nicodemus* his name was Dismas, which comes from the Greek for "sunset" or "death." He is on Christ's right, to show that he is with the blessed sheep at the right hand of God (Mt 25:31-46).

In small print next to his head is Ukrainian text that reads, "Remember me, Lord." This is the beginning of his sublime plea for mercy, a plea which we commemorate—and a sentiment which we echo—with every Prayer Before Holy Communion.

The evil thief, known from the same apocryphal source as Gestas, is on Christ's left, indicating that he is *presumably* with the selfish goats, cast "into everlasting fire which was prepared for the devil and his angels" (Mt 25:41). Although the Church teaches that there are people in hell and that their punishment is eternal, we cannot know what transpires in a person's soul at the instant of death, and thus the Church in her wisdom does not officially pronounce the damnation of any specific persons, including Gestas. Though we strive to maintain some small measure of hope for his salvation, his story is still a grave reminder that we must be faithful to Christ and accept His mercy.

The thieves are not nailed to their crosses, as is Christ. Historically, this may have occurred because the executioners reserved their especial cruelty for Our Lord, but the spiritual message in the icon is that the Christian must cling to his own cross as his surest ladder to heaven. Together the Savior and the other two crucifieds present a hierarchy of adhesion: Christ is *nailed* in perfect resignation, the good thief is *thrice tied down* yet sorrowful, but the bad thief is simply *tied once* around the legs and he scowls in irritation—he does not accept his cross.

The Groups of Three, and the Mourners

The composition is arranged in several groups of three figures, with some figures belonging to more than one group.

Most noticeably, Christ forms a group of three with the two crucified criminals. The Roman soldiers form another, as do the three female mourners. Another group of three formed by two of the soldiers along with John visually parallels the female mourners. A further triad is formed of three groups: the three victims of crucifixion, the Romans whose heads are all roughly level, and all four of the mourners who are at the same level in the icon. Less obviously, there are three groups according to sanctity: Christ the God-Man, then the spotless Virgin and the company of nimbate saints, and lastly the trio of sinners—Dismas, and the men with sponge and lance.

Yet the most important group of three is composed of Christ, Mary, and John. This is the supreme triangle of love in the icon: Our Lord gives His beloved mother to John, and through John to the whole Church; the Apostle looks to the Lady, and she in turn looks up to her Son, who, though here deceased, still faces toward them both. So also does Mary always lead the faithful Catholic closer to the divine Lamb.

The Romans and the Spear

To the center left, another shield-bearing man, wearing a simplified version of a Roman Imperial Gallic helmet without plume, wields the lance that pierces Christ's side. John 19:34 says that a soldier pierced Christ's side, and Mark 15:29 notes that a centurion converted, but these two individuals are not explicitly identified as the same person. The *Gospel of Nicodemus*, however, indicates that both events involve a person known as Longinus.

The converting centurion, right, gestures as he says, "Indeed this man was the son of God" (Mk 15:39). Be he the same soldier as lanced Our Lord or not, Longinus is nonetheless honored as a saint and martyr by the Catholic Church.

Although the entire Passion and Resurrection of Christ are re-presented during the Divine Liturgy, His Crucifixion, and most especially His being pierced by a lance, are explicitly commemorated before the public ceremony begins in what is called the *Liturgy of Preparation*.

At the prothesis, the small table to the worshipper's left, before every Divine Liturgy the priest blesses the prosphoron, the bread to be consecrated into the Eucharist, and he begins the preparation by praying,

> O God, cleanse me, a sinner, and have mercy on me. By thy precious Blood Thou hast redeemed us
> from the curse of the law. By being nailed to the Cross and pierced with a spear, Thou hast poured
> immortality upon men. O our Savior, glory to Thee!

On the prothesis lies a liturgical spear, in commemoration of the lance of Longinus, and the priest will first use this to pierce the side of the prosphoron; then, invoking the Crucifixion, the Mother of God, the righteous who lived before Christ, and the saints of the Church, the priest cuts the prosphoron into cubes suitable for the Eucharist.

The Roman and the Sponge

To the center right, the man with the sponge is also most likely Roman, as his leggings show that he is not Jewish; as Jews are almost always depicted wearing sandals, with a few exceptions for the poor and certain laborers.

The hyssop sponge is important because it connects Christ's sacrifice to the hyssop used to sprinkle blood on the doors for Passover (Ex 12:22) and to the ritual sacrifices of the Old Law (Lv 14; Nm 19). During the Divine Liturgy, after the Eucharist, a liturgical sponge is used to purify the sacred vessels, in remembrance of the hyssop offered to Christ.

Adam in Hades

The Ukrainian near the skull translates to "Head of Adam." Around it is written a lamentation for what was lost: "Here once was a paradise." In Hades, Adam is distraught, repentant for his sins, his brow furrowed; he suffers from the death he called down upon mankind yet awaits new life in the opening of the kingdom of heaven.

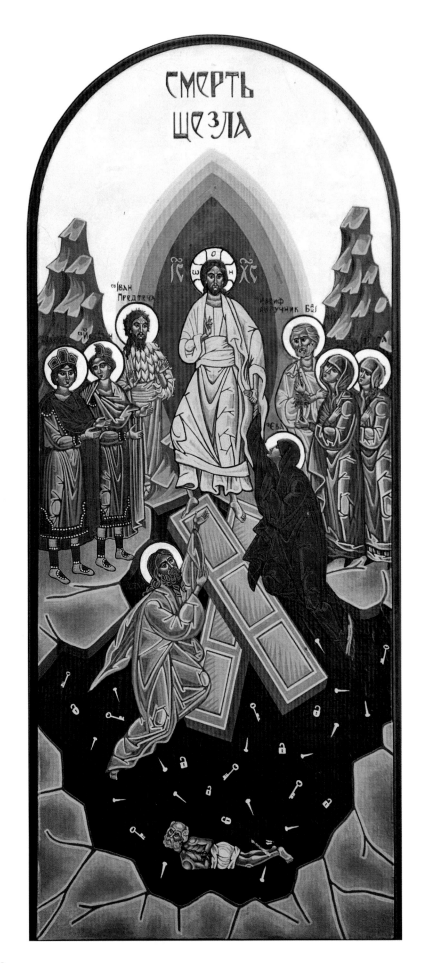

The Anastasis

This icon's name is from the Greek for "Resurrection," although the events depicted are more closely linked to the rebirth of fallen mankind than to the Resurrection in the flesh of Our Lord.

It is also known as *Descent into Hades*, or, in a vivid and charming traditional English description, *Harrowing of Hell*.

"Death reigned from Adam unto Moses" (Rom 5:14), and those virtuous deceased who were in the prison of death had been "incredulous," as they "waited for the patience of God" (1 Pt 3:20) to reveal His merciful plan to come to their aid.

Christ smashes the doors of Hades that hold them captive and rescues them from the abode of the dead (Eph 4:8-10). The locks that bound humanity to the netherworld fall harmlessly into the black. The personification of death is now depicted as an old man—fettered, angry, and powerless.

An immense mandorla emanates from Christ, proclaiming His majesty and show that the other world is breaking into ours. This light is also the intense illumination of the Savior, who has defeated death (2 Tm 1:10).

Adam and Eve—the first humans to sin and thus those responsible for our exile (Gn 3)—reach up for Christ's saving grasp, and Our Lord has already taken Eve by the wrist.

Christ looks directly out to the worshipper, speaking to him, and He makes a gesture of teaching, beckoning the viewer to see His glory and learn of the New Life He has won for us.

To our left, Christ's righteous ancestors, David and Solomon, and His close kinsman, John the Forerunner, express their amazement at this sublime rescue. To our right, Joseph the Betrothed, the prophetess Debbora, and Christ's foremother Ruth hold attributes related to their holy lives; their hands are to their hearts and they bear expressions of love and devotion.

Christ, and Adam and Eve

The Old Adam and the New Adam (1 Cor 15:45) meet face-to-face.

Christ's hands and feet now show the glorious wounds He acquired during His victorious battle. The broken doors of Hades lie crosswise, an allusion to the weapon with which Our Lord defeated the power of death.

The triumphant Son of God is robed in shining white garments, as in the Transfiguration (Lk 9:29), and they are punctuated with golden assiste, which especially radiate His divine holiness.

Feast Day:
Pascha, the Bright Resurrection of Christ

Troparion, Tone V:
Christ is risen from the dead * trampling death by death * and to those in the tombs giving life.

Daily Tropar - Sunday:
The Resurrection

Troparion, Tone II:
When You went down to death, O Life Immortal, * You struck Hades dead with the blazing light of Your divinity. * You raised the dead from the nether world, * all the powers of heaven cried out: * "O Giver of Life, Christ our God, glory be to You!"

In most icons of this type, the flutter of Christ's robes makes it evident that He is descending and not ascending, but no particular directionality can be discerned in this example. However, it is important to note that *Anastasis* does not depict His physical Resurrection from death, which would be an ascent, but instead His downward movement into the netherworld to rescue the departed.

All that Adam and Eve can do to escape death is reach up—it is Christ who grabs Eve by the wrist and pulls her to salvation. Similarly, the Christian can only seek out and cooperate with divine grace, for only Christ our God can actually merit our salvation.

The entire icon radiates Christ's profound strength, activity, manliness, and heroism.

Righteous Departed

Ruth, the Gentile Moabite maiden who joined the people of Israel, carries a small sheaf of wheat from the fields of Booz (Ru 3-4), who would later become her husband. Together they are great-grandparents of King David. Booz is a type of Christ, in that he weds himself to a Gentile and therefore permanently joins her to the community of salvation, as Our Lord wed Himself to the Gentiles in His Church.

Debbora presents a small palm tree, like the one under which she sat and prophesied; "the children of Israel came up to her for all judgment" (Jgs 4:5).

Joseph holds a lily, in accordance with a scene from the *Protoevangelion of James*: The high priest declares that Mary's future spouse will be chosen from among the bachelors of the house of David. They will bring their walking sticks to the altar, and the one from whose stick a flower blooms and upon which a dove alights will be Mary's husband. Joseph, being older, did not participate, and no one fulfilled the expectations. Joseph was then persuaded to participate; his rod bloomed and a dove perched upon it, whereupon he was betrothed to Our Lady.

Royally clad to the left are David and Solomon, kings of the united Israel and two of Christ's most illustrious ancestors. The less-perfect Solomon can be distinguished by his broken half-crown and his turned-away face, which establishes his moral inferiority to David in that he, the wisest of men (3 Kgs 3), turned away from the Lord for a time and worshipped the false idols of his pagan wives (3 Kgs 11).

John has his curly hair and wears his rough addereth hairshirt. He is believed to have been Christ's forerunner in Hades, as he was on earth, declaring to the dead that Christ would come to set them free.

Hades and Death

Anastasis makes much use of *allegory*, that is, it depicts abstract and spiritual meanings in material forms. Hades did not actually have physical doors, nor did death reign in the personage of an old man.

Hades, we must remember, was at this time the abode of all the dead, and so the righteous also were there awaiting salvation. Consequently, the image does not depict the hell of the damned, or "the Pit" (Mt 15:14; Apoc 9), and thus it lacks "hellish" characteristics such as flames, allegorical monsters, and fallen angels.

Rather, this Hades is a holding cell, a place that would have been an eternal spiritual twilight for its occupants if Christ had not smashed its gates and set them free.

In the *Gospel of Nicodemus*, the personification of Hades bewails that he recently was forced to give up Lazarus at the command of the Savior, and he asks the evil one to not have Our Lord killed so that Hades will not be plundered of more souls. But the proud fallen angel is confident that they can hold out against Jesus, and so Hades bids his retainers to resist Christ and to secure the bolts and bars of the gates. But it is all in vain—when the King of Glory came to Hades, all the dark places were set alight. After Christ's descent, there remained no place to which the Light of God had not shone.

As the Icon of Pascha

The Descent into Hades was commenced by Christ immediately upon His death on Holy Friday, and thus on Holy Saturday it is liturgically commemorated in a special way.

However, the central theme of *Anastasis*—the salvation of fallen humanity—is fundamental to the meaning and celebration of Pascha; since there is no traditional and widely venerated icon precisely depicting Christ's Resurrection *in the flesh* on Pascha, *Anastasis* is not only connected to Holy Saturday but also considered the Paschal icon par excellence.

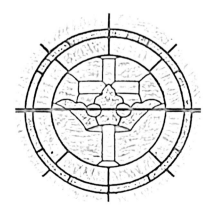

Appendices

While it is perhaps not at all worthy of your expectation, it is yet the best I could do. ... Perhaps it might happen that something useful to the soul will be revealed out of them.

-St. Maximus the Confessor
Four Hundred Chapters on Love, circa AD 626

Appendix I: Other Icons

Two additional icons are included here for the sake of completeness. The first is *Ascension*, the only one of the Twelve Great Feasts not numbered among the permanent icons of St. Nicholas Church.

The other is the icon of *All Saints*, in order to have liturgical propers from each day of the week.

The photo of *Ascension* is taken from the collection of smaller icons that are placed for the veneration of the faithful on the *tetrapod*, the small table near the front of the nave, and which are chosen to accord with the nearest feast day.

Feast Day:
Ascension of Our Lord - Forty Days after Pascha

Kontakion, Tone VI:
When You had fulfilled Your plan for us * and united things on earth with those in heaven, * You ascended in glory, O Christ our God, * in no way distant, but remaining insep'rable, * You cried to those who love You: * I am with You and there is none against you.

The Ascension

Christ remained on earth for forty days after His Resurrection, appearing to the Apostles and instructing them in His doctrine and the nature of their evangelical mission. They ask Him when Israel will be restored. He replies,

> It is not for you to know the times or moments, which the Father hath put in his own power: But you shall receive the power of the Holy Ghost coming upon you, and you shall be witnesses unto me in Jerusalem, and in all Judea, and Samaria, and even to the uttermost part of the earth. And when he had said these things, while they looked on, he was raised up: and a cloud received him out of their sight (Acts 1:7-9).

While they watch Him ascend, two angels appear as men dressed in white and approach them, saying, "Ye men of Galilee, why stand you looking up to heaven? This Jesus who is taken up from you into heaven, shall so come, as you have seen him going into heaven" (Acts 1:11).

All Saints

Weekday Troparia - Saturday, All Saints and the Faithful Departed

Troparion to All Saints, Tone II:
Apostles, prophets, martyrs, bishops, venerable and righteous ones, * having finished the fight well and having kept the faith, * you now have free approach to the Savior. * For our sake, we beseech you, * entreat Him in His goodness to save our souls.

Troparion for the Faithful Departed, Tone II:
Remember Your servants, O Lord, * because of Your goodness, and forgive all the sins they committed in life, * for no one is sinless but You, * Who alone can give rest to the departed.

Appendix II: Afterword

Even a quick glimpse at the icons in St. Nicholas Church will reveal the *universality* of the iconographic tradition. The Greek, Ukrainian, and Hebrew languages mix freely and commingle with classical Greco-Roman artistic forms, and with clothing and hairstyles drawn from medieval Kyivan Rus', the Hebrews, and other peoples of the Near East.

Not all forms of sacred art exhibit this blessed catholicity. Many, though strikingly beautiful, are clearly the products of specific times and places; these eventually become passé or quaint, at which point they are more suitable to be hung in a museum than for active devotion. Iconography, however, despite passing through the hands of many different nations, remains firmly rooted in Late Antique culture—the time of the Fathers of the Church, an era when Christendom became nearly synonymous with the Roman Empire, itself a multicultural and international institution.

This character of universality and antiquity extends beyond iconography to the other practices of the Greek Catholic churches which are beyond the scope of this book—liturgical texts and rituals, vestments and the practical arts, chant, and other traditions. For these reasons, the Greek Catholic inheritance has a profound ability to help a man transcend that time and place in which he happens to be and then grasp upward for something larger—that prodigious communion of believers in Christ Jesus composed of those who went before him, those who live now in other parts of the world, and those yet to come in future ages in every corner of the world.

Indeed, the more crude, banal, and ephemeral one's larger culture becomes, the more compelling is the timelessness of the Greek Catholic Church.

May God in His mercy grant to the United States men and women who, like Saints Cyril and Methodius, are willing to translate this ancient patrimony into the conversion of the entire nation.

Glory Be To Jesus Christ!

Appendix III: The Bible

The Holy Bible. Douay-Rheims (Challoner) Version. John Murphy Company, 1899. Imprimatur: James Cardinal Gibbons, Archbishop of Baltimore, September 1, 1899. Print. Available online at http://www.drbo.org.

The New Testament. Douay-Rheims (Confraternity) Version. Patterson, NJ: St. Anthony Guild Press, 1941. Imprimatur: Most Rev. Thomas H. McLaughlin, S.T.D., Bishop of Patterson. Print.

Note About Versions

The Psalms and their numbers, and the names of some books and persons, are given herein according to the *Septuagint*, the original Greek-language version of the Old Testament. It was translated circa 150 BC by 72 Hebrew elders and was the version most commonly quoted by Christ and the Apostles. It is also the basis of the Slavonic translation and, to a significant degree, of the Latin Vulgate, which is the primary source of the English translations used in this book.

Consequently, the Psalm numbers and many of the proper names in this book are slightly different from those of modern Bible translations that rely on Protestant and medieval Hebrew editions.

Although the sacred English of the Challoner Douay-Rheims edition has enduring value, in certain places the more recent Confraternity Version of the Douay-Rheims is used to enhance readability. These are noted *CV*.

Citations and Alternate Names

Only those books that have been cited are listed. For the convenience of those using other translations, alternate versions of names are given in parentheses.

Old Testament

Legal Books
Gn - Genesis
Ex - Exodus
Lv - Leviticus Nm - Numbers
Dt - Deuteronomy

Historical Books
Jo - Josue (Joshua)
Jgs - Judges
1 Kgs - 1 Kings (1 Samuel)

2 Kgs - 2 Kings (2 Samuel)
3 Kgs - 3 Kings (1 Kings)
4 Kgs - 4 Kings (2 Kings)
Tb - Tobias (Tobit)

Sapiential Books
Jb - Job
Ps - Psalms
Prv - Proverbs
Can - Canticle of Canticles (Song of Songs, Song of Solomon)
Ecclus - Ecclesiasticus (Wisdom of Sirach)

Prophetic Books
Is - Isaias (Isaiah)
Jer - Jeremias (Jeremiah)
Bar - Baruch
Ez - Ezechiel (Ezeckiel, Ezekiel)
Dn - Daniel
Jl - Joel
Hab - Habacuc (Habakkuk)
Zac - Zacharias (Zachariah)
Mal - Malachias (Malachi)

Machabees
1 Mc - 1 Machabees (1 Maccabees)
2 Mc - 2 Machabees (2 Maccabees)

New Testament

Gospels
Mt - Matthew
Mk - Mark
Lk - Luke
Jn - John

Acts
Acts - Acts of the Apostles

Epistles
Rom - Romans
1 Cor - 1 Corinthians
2 Cor - 2 Corinthians
Gal - Galatians
Eph - Ephesians
Phil - Philippians
1 Tm - 1 Timothy
2 Tm - 2 Timothy
Heb - Hebrews
Jas - James
1 Pt - 1 Peter
Jude - Jude

Apocalypse
Apoc - Apocalypse (Revelation)

Appendix IV: Bibliography

Please note that not all of the below are from perfectly orthodox Catholic sources or authors. In all things care must be taken to separate the wheat from the chaff.

And just as in culling roses we avoid the thorns, from such writings as these we
will gather everything useful, and guard against the noxious.

—St. Basil the Great
Address to Young Men on the Right Use of Greek Literature

Note About Propers

For almost every proper, the *Anthology for Worship* was used. If that source did not have the propers, the books put out by the Sisters of St. Basil were used. These are marked *SB*, and as it happens, are all from the *Festal Menaion*. When the Basilian texts also lacked the propers (or in one case when they were difficult to understand), the Holy Trinity Parish website's *Orthodox Calendar* was used. These last are marked *HT*—and as an extra benefit they are in a delightfully flavorful sacred English.

Liturgical Texts

Divine Liturgy: An Anthology for Worship. Ed. Peter Galadza, et al. Ottawa, ON, Canada: Metropolitan Andrey Sheptytsky Institute of Eastern Christian Studies, 2004. Print.

The Divine Liturgy of Saint John Chrysostom. Philadelphia, PA: Synod of the Hierarchy of the Ukrainian Catholic Church, 1988. Print.

Divine Office. Compiled and translated, Basilian Fathers of Glen Cove, NY. Stamford, CT: 2003. Print.

Festal Menaion. Compiled and adapted, Liturgical Commission of the Sisters of St. Basil the Great. Uniontown, PA: January 1, 1985. Print.

Lenten Triodion. Compiled and adapted, Liturgical Commission of the Sisters of St. Basil the Great. Uniontown, PA: 1995. Print.

Orthodox Calendar. Compiled, Holy Trinity Russian Orthodox Church. Baltimore, MD. www.holytrinityorthodox.com.

Pentecostarion. Compiled and adapted, Liturgical Commission of the Sisters of St. Basil the Great. Uniontown, PA: May 18, 1986. Print.

Primary Icon Texts

Coomler, David. *The Icon Handbook*. Springfield, IL: Templegate Publishers, 1995. Print.

Dionysius of Fourna. *The "Painter's Manual" of Dionysius of Fourna*. Trans. Paul Hetherington. Torrance, CA: Oakwood Publications, 1996. Print.

Evdokimov, Fr. Michael. *Light from the East: Icons in Liturgy and Prayer*. Trans. Br. Robert Smith, F.S.C. Mahwah, NJ: Paulist Press, 2004. Print.

Haustein-Bartsch, Eva. *Icons*. Ed. Norbert Wolf. Cologne, Germany: Taschen, 2008. Print.

Martin, Linette. *Sacred Doorways: A Beginner's Guide to Icons*. Brewster, MA: Paraclete Press, 2002. Print.

Nes, Solrunn. *The Mysical Language of Icons*. Grand Rapids, MI, and Cambridge, UK: William B. Eerdmans Publishing Company, 2004. Print.

Ouspensky, Leonid and Vladimir Lossky. *The Meaning of Icons*. Crestwood, NY: St. Vladimir's Seminary Press, 1999. Print.

Tradigo, Alfredo. *Icons and Saints of the Eastern Orthodox Church*. Trans. Stephen Sartarelli. Los Angeles, CA: Getty Publications, 2006 (English). Print.

Apocryphal Gospels

Gospel of Nicodemus, or *Acts of Pilate*. Original, before AD 376. Revised, Middle Ages.

Protoevangelion of James. Circa AD 145.

Pseudo-Matthew. *The Book About the Origin of the Blessed Mary and the Childhood of the Savior*, or *The Gospel of Pseudo-Matthew*. Circa AD 575.

Other Useful Texts

Bigham, Steven. *Heroes of the Icon*. Torrance, CA: Oakwood Publications, 1998. Print.

Dribnenky, Bernard Basil. *The Year of Eternity*. Toronto, ON, Canada: Basilian Press, 1994. Print.

Eusebius of Caesaria. *Ecclesiastical History*. Trans. C. F. Cruse. Peabody, MA: Hendrickson Publishers, Inc., 1998. Print.

John of Damascus. *Apologia of St. John of Damascus Against Those Who Decry Holy Images*. London, England: Thomas Baker, 1898. Republished, Grand Rapids, MI: Christian Classics Ethereal Library, 2001. www.ccel.org/ccel/damascus/icons.html.

Justin Martyr. *Dialogue with Trypho*. Second century. Trans. Thomas B. Falls. Washington, DC: Catholic University of America Press; Revised Edition, July 1, 2003.

Nestor the Chronicler. *The Tale of Bygone Years*, or *Primary Chronicle*. Circa AD 1113.

Peck, Fr. John A. *Divine Liturgy: A Student Study Text*. John A. Peck, 1995. Reprinted, Lexington, KY: Interior Strength Press, 2012. Print.

Salza, John. *The Biblical Basis for Tradition*. Fairfield, NJ: ACLA Press, 2010. Print. Nota Bene: Chapter 6, *The Canon of Scripture* and Chapter 7, *The Deuterocanonical Books*.

Schaff, Philip, ed. *The Seven Ecumenical Councils*. Edinburgh, Scotland: T&T Clark. Late nineteenth century. Republished, Grand Rapids, MI: Christian Classics Ethereal Library. www.ccel.org/ccel/schaff/npnf214.html.

St. Nicholas Ukrainian Catholic Church. *1907-2007 Centennial Book*. Schenectady, NY: Allegra Print & Imaging, 2007. Print.

Union of Brest. 1595. http://www.stjosaphatugcc.org/full-text-of-the-union-of-brest.php.

Appendix V: Iconographers

Dochwat, Christina. Iconostasis and side shrines. Philadelphia, PA. 1964.

Drozda, Ann. Free-hanging festal and biblical scenes, and iconostasis apostle tier. Pittsfield, MA. 1982.

Makarenko, Sviatoslav of Makarenko Studios. Apse and sanctuary. Yonkers, NY. 2006.

Markovych, Roman of MarkArt. Nave walls, vault, *Chi-Rho, Greek Cross, Mystical Supper* on iconostasis, and patterning around upper side shrines. Stamford, CT. 2006-07, except for *Jeremias* and *Ezechiel*, 2012.

Appendix VI: Icons By Church Year

Immoveable Feasts

Page	Feast Day	Icon (or Entry)	Date
3	Indiction	*Christ Pantocrator*	September 1
39	Moses	*Moses*	September 4
67	Nativity of the Mother of God	*Nativity of the Mother of God*	September 8
18	Exaltation of the Holy Cross	*Globus Cruciger*	September 14
49	Protection of the Mother of God	*Protection of the Mother of God*	October 1
31	Thomas	*Thomas*	October 6
34	James of Alphaeus	*James of Alphaeus*	October 9
10	Luke	*Luke*	October 18
25	Michael and All Angels	*Michael*	November 8
58	Josaphat	*Josaphat*	November 12
30	Philip	*Philip*	November 14
10	Matthew	*Matthew* (Vault)	November 16
35	Matthew	*Matthew* (Iconostasis)	November 16
70	Presentation	*Presentation*	November 21
61	Dedication of St. George	*Cathedral of St. George*	November 27
31	Andrew	*Andrew*	November 30
51	Nicholas	*Nicholas*	December 6
44	Daniel	*Daniel*	December 17
89	Nativity of Our Lord	*Nativity of Our Lord*	December 25
21	Synaxis of the Mother of God	*Mother of God Hodegetria*	December 26
27	Stephen	*Stephen*	December 27
93	Theophany	*Theophany*	January 6
77	Holy Meeting	*Holy Meeting*	February 2
72	Annunciation	*Annunciation*	March 25
10	Mark	*Mark*	April 25
30	James of Zebedee	*James of Zebedee*	April 30
38	Jeremias	*Jeremias*	May 1
10	John	*John* (Vault)	May 8
32	John	*John* (Iconostasis)	May 8
40	Isaias	*Isaias*	May 9
34	Simon the Zealot	*Simon the Zealot*	May 10
56	Dedication of St. Sophia	*Cathedral of St. Sophia*	May 11
54	Constantine and Helena	*Chi-Rho*	May 21
35	Bartholomew	*Bartholomew*	June 11
33	Jude	*Jude*	June 19
32/33	Peter and Paul	*Peter and Paul*	June 29
29	Synaxis of the Twelve Apostles	The Twelve Apostles	June 30

52	Olha	*Olha*	July 11
52	Vladimir	*Vladimir*	July 15
43	Elias	*Elias*	July 20
45	Ezechiel	*Ezechiel*	July 21
108	Transfiguration	*Transfiguration*	August 6
76	Matthias	Matthias detail (with *Dormition*)	August 9
74	Dormition	*Dormition*	August 15

Moveable Feasts

Page	Feast Day	Icon (or Entry)	Day
18	Sunday of Orthodoxy	*Christ the Teacher*	1st Sunday of Great Lent
6	Akathist Saturday	*Mother of God Platytera*	5th Saturday of Great Lent
41	Holy Forefathers	*Solomon*	Sunday between December 11 and 17
42	David, Joseph, and James	*David*	Sunday after the Nativity of Christ
112	Lazarus Saturday	*Raising of Lazarus*	6th Saturday of Great Lent
122	Palm Sunday	*Entrance into Jerusalem*	6th Sunday of Great Lent
23	Holy Thursday	*Mystical Supper* (Iconostasis)	Holy Thursday
130	Holy Thursday	*Mystical Supper* (Wall Feast)	Holy Thursday
132	Holy Friday	*Crucifixion*	Holy Friday
79	Holy Friday	*Descent from the Cross*	Holy Friday
136	Pascha	*Anastasis*	Pascha
126	Bright Friday	*Christ Cleanses the Temple*	Bright Friday
98	2nd Monday of Pascha	*Wedding Feast at Cana*	2nd Monday of Pascha
81	3rd Sunday of Pascha	*Myrrh-Bearing Women*	3rd Sunday of Pascha
102	5th Sunday of Pascha	*Samaritan Woman*	5th Sunday of Pascha
115	Man Born Blind	*Man Born Blind* (with *Lazarus*)	6th Sunday of Pascha
142	Ascension	*Ascension* (Other Icons)	Forty days after Pascha
83	Descent of the Holy Spirit	*Descent of the Holy Spirit*	Fifty days after Pascha
104	9th Sunday after Pentecost	*Christ Walks on Water*	9th Sunday after Pentecost
116	12th Sunday after Pentecost	*Rich Young Man*	12th Sunday after Pentecost
121	31st Sunday after Pentecost	*Blind Man* (with *Zacheus*)	31st Sunday after Pentecost
118	37th Sunday after Pentecost	*Calling of Zacheus*	37th Sunday after Pentecost

Weekday Propers

Page	Commemoration	Icon (or Entry)	Day
136	Resurrection	*Anastasis*	Sunday
8	All Holy Angels	Angels detail (with *Mother of God Platytera*)	Monday
95	John the Forerunner	John the Forerunner detail (with *Theophany*)	Tuesday
60	Cross	*Cross*	Wednesday
29	Apostles	Twelve Apostles	Thursday
51	St. Nicholas	*Nicholas*	Thursday
60	Cross	*Cross*	Friday
143	All Saints	*All Saints* (Other Icons)	Saturday

Appendix VII: Glossary

Addereth (from Hebrew *cloak* or *glory*)**:** The rough, hairy cloak worn by Saints John the Forerunner and Elias.

Adventus (from Latin *approach*)**:** A type of classical art that celebrates the triumphal entrance of an emperor into a city.

Allegory: The use of people or events to represent ideas or concepts.

Altar (from Latin *burning place*)**:** The cube in the sanctuary of the church on which the Eucharistic sacrifice takes place.

Ambon (from Greek *step*)**:** The elevated walkway in front of the iconostasis. Also called an *ambo*.

Amphora (plural *amphorae*)**:** An early type of jug used to hold water, wine, and other liquids. Usually ceramic with two handles.

Anastasis (from Greek *resurrection*)**:** See icon entry.

Apocrypha: Non-scriptural accounts of the lives of Christ and other biblical figures. They are not accepted as the Word of God, but this does not mean they lack value. A few of them became sources for iconographic scenes.

Aposticha (from Greek *hymns on the verses*)**:** A type of hymn chanted near the end of vespers and matins.

Apse (from Greek *arch*)**:** The hemispheric ceiling above the sanctuary.

Arc of Heaven: An aureole that depicts someone in heaven taking action on earth. Usually semicircular, dark blue, and near the top of an icon. Frequently contains a *Manus Dei* or Christ in Glory.

Archetype (from Greek *first model*)**:** The person represented in an icon. Veneration directed through the icon is actually given to this person. Also called the *prototype*.

Acheiropoieton (from Greek *not made by hands*)**:** Any icon that is believed to have been created miraculously by God. Famous examples include the original *Mandylion*, the *Shroud of Turin*, and the original *Virgin of Guadalupe*.

Assiste: Highlighting, typically of gold, worked into the clothing of a saint to show that he reflects the Light of God, or into the garments of Christ because He is the Light of God.

Attribute: An item carried by or placed near a person that identifies him. For example, St. Andrew's saltire cross or St. Peter's keys.

Aureole (from Latin *golden*)**:** A stylized area of light that either represents personal sanctity and emanates from a holy person or represents the in-breaking of the heavenly realm into our world.

Baldachin (from Italian *Baghdad cloth*)**:** Any of various types of canopies over royalty, or over an altar or other holy places; usually on four pillars. Permanent fixed versions over altars are usually called *ciboria*.

Beards: Typically used to show the age of the wearer. A beardless man is a youth or very young adult; scruff, called an *incipient beard*, indicates early manhood. A full-but-short beard often means the gentleman is in the prime of his life. Longer beards may indicate age, wisdom, penance, or monastic status. Jewish priests in icons also wear long beards. Knotty and unkempt beards most commonly indicate that the wearer has a penitential lifestyle, or occasionally that he is poor.

Bema (from Greek *step*): The entire raised floor at the eastern end of the church, containing both the ambon and the sanctuary floor.

Buskins: Ornate liturgical shoes, descended from the courtly attire of Constantinople and now rarely used.

Celestial Sphere: The whole of Creation, heaven and earth. Often depicted in icons as a *globus*.

Chi-rho: Any of the christograms made from the first two letters of Christ's name in Greek: X and P, chi and rho.

Chiton (from Greek *tunic*): The most common inner tunic worn in iconography.

Chlamys: A type of cloak, usually worn by the military, that clasps at the neck to allow access to a sword and that may be wrapped around the forearm as a light shield.

Christogram: Any monogram of Christ. Common christograms include the chi-rho and the IHS popular in the Latin Church.

Ciborium (plural *ciboria*): A permanent architectural canopy over an altar or other holy place, usually on four pillars.

Clavus (plural *clavi*): A stripe of color on a person's robe indicating his rank, usually around the shoulder or arm. Common in Ancient Roman secular government and adapted to iconography to convey the dignity of the wearer.

Codex (from Latin *block of wood*; plural *codices*): An early style of book frequently seen in iconography. The pages are the same height as the covers and there is no spine—before people owned numerous books, they stored them flat and thus had no need for spine titles.

Colobium: A rectangular, sleeveless tunic that covered both shoulders, sometimes tied at the waist.

Condensed Time: The representation of several events together in the same scene, even if they did not literally occur together, so as to tell a whole story in a single image, or to provide more signification, or to make manifest the eternal Now of the icon. Also called *simultaneous narration*.

Constantinople: First the co-capital and then the sole capital of the Roman Empire for 1,123 years, from its dedication under St. Constantine the Great in AD 330 until it was conquered and plundered in AD 1453. It was also the patriarchal seat of the Greek Rite churches. Much of the visual language of iconography comes from its imperial court. Interestingly, the multicultural Roman Empire was governed by Greco-Romans from Constantinople for twice as long as it was governed by Latin Romans from the city of Rome.

Cosmos (from Greek *order*): An elderly king holding twelve scrolls; the *personification* of old sinful humanity.

Crozier: The staff carried by bishops and other high-ranking clerics as a symbol of their office.

Dalmatic (from Latin *of Dalmatia*): A type of tunic once worn by members of the imperial court in Constantinople and now frequently seen in iconography worn by angels or royalty. Also a liturgical garment in the Latin Church similar to the *sticharion*, though not typically seen this way in iconography.

Deacon's Doors: The two doors on the north and south sides of the iconostasis.

Death: In iconography, an old man who is a *personification* of spiritual death and separation from God, usually shown defeated by Christ and bound.

Decalogue (from Greek *ten words*): The Ten Commandments.

Deisis (from Greek *supplication*): Any of several types of icons in which Christ is at the center, usually enthroned or otherwise glorified and flanked by the Mother of God and John the Forerunner bowing to Him. Different versions may have other saints behind these two.

Diakonikon: The small room to the worshipper's right of the sanctuary; it holds vestments and sacred vessels and is typically maintained by the deacon.

Divitision: A silk tunic, usually belted; worn by members of the Eastern Roman court and often by distinguished persons in icons.

Dodekaorton: The Twelve Great Feasts of the Church.

Dome: A hemispherical ceiling in a church. Contrast: *vault*.

Dulia (from Greek *veneration*): The worship of honor paid to all noble things, including saints and icons. These things are good not in themselves but insofar as they participate in the ultimate Good who is God. Contrast: *latria*.

Emmanuel (from Hebrew *God with us*): A depiction of Christ as a boy who looks like a small adult; used to emphasize the Incarnation.

Ephod (from Hebrew *to put on*): The liturgical apron worn by Israel's high priest underneath his breastplate, the *hoshen*.

Epimanikion (plural *epimanikia*): Liturgical wrist cuffs used to keep the sticharion in place.

Epithet (from Greek *attributed*): A description that becomes attached to a person's name in common usage, as in St. Nicholas the Wonderworker. They are positive descriptions, not negative ones as in the common modern use of the term. Sometimes called an *appellation*.

Epitrachelion (from Greek *over the neck*): The long, narrow band of fabric worn around the shoulders by priests and bishops as a symbol of their priesthood.

Epistyle (from Greek *door frame*): In general, the molding above a doorway, especially one made of columns. Specifically, the place on the iconostasis above the Royal Doors where the Mystical Supper is placed. Also called an *architrave*.

Fibula (from Latin *clasp* or *brooch*): A clasp, typically used to hold two ends of a cloak together around the neck.

Fillet (from Old French *thread* or *strip*): A hair tie, formerly worn in the Near East to mark a woman as not married; in the case of angels, to note their lack of fleshly reproduction.

Globus (from Latin *orb*): Any of various spheres held by Christ or others that symbolize His dominion. It represents the whole sphere of the cosmos, not merely the globe of the earth.

Globus Cruciger (from Latin *cross-bearing orb*): A globus topped with a cross.

Greek Cross: A cross with two bars of equal length set in the middle of each other.

Hades of the Fathers: The abode of the righteous departed before Christ's Resurrection opened the gates of heaven.

Hades of the Damned: The permanent place of punishment for those who die separated from God's love. Synonymous with the common English-language term "hell."

Halo (from Greek *disc of the sun or moon*): See *nimbus*.

Hierarchical Perspective: A non-naturalistic perspective in which the figures who are more holy or more important are drawn on a larger scale and the figures who are less holy or less important are drawn on a smaller scale.

Himation: The most common outer cloak appearing in iconography.

Hodegetria (from Greek *she who shows the way*): An *epithet* of the Mother of God. See icon entry.

Hoshen: The breastplate worn by Israel's high priest on which were laid twelve precious stones, each engraved with the name of a tribe of Israel.

Hyperdulia: The special worship of honor paid to the Mother of God. It differs from *dulia* in degree.

Iconoclasm (from Greek *image breaking*): A heresy that condemns religious imagery as idolatrous. Conclusively defeated in orthodox Catholicism by the Second Council of Nicaea in AD 787, but still present in Islam and certain Protestant communities.

Iconostasis (from Greek *image stand*): The icon screen that unites the sanctuary and the nave. The iconostasis is a development that parallels the altar rail in Latin-rite churches; both originate from the Greek *templon*, a low wall around the sanctuary.

Iconodulia (from Greek *image veneration*): The theological movement which defended religious images from their opponents. Also called *iconophilia*.

Inconsistent Perspective: The intentional depiction of a thing in an unrealistic and sometimes physically impossible manner; used to emphasize the thing's symbolic importance over its physical reality.

Irmos (from Greek *series*): A certain type of hymn used during liturgies. Also called a *Hirmos*.

Jordan: In iconography, an old man that is a personification of the Jordan River, shown under water and usually carrying a jug from which the river pours.

Kairos (from Greek *supreme time*): A term that means "in the perfect time of God" or "outside of time" or "the in-breaking of eternity into time"; the Divine Liturgy and iconography provide opportunities to experience it.

Kekryphalos: A hair-gathering coif at one time worn by Syrian and other Near Eastern married women; worn by the Virgin and other married women in icons under their *maphoria*.

Kerygma (from Greek *proclamation*): The process by which the Holy Spirit impresses Himself onto a soul and reworks it in His image. It continues steadily through the life of a faithful Catholic, and is especially strong during prayer and reception of the Holy Mysteries. Prayer before and contemplation of icons open the worshipper to it.

Kontakion (from Greek *pole* (on which a scroll is wound); plural *kontakia*): A liturgical hymn relating to the feast or saint of the day. In days gone by they were quite long; now they are usually abbreviated. Often called a *kontak* (plural *kontaki*) in churches of Slavic tradition.

Lacerna: A rough woolen cloak of barbarian origin, popularized by Roman soldiers fighting in cold, wet climates.

Late Antiquity: The era of Greco-Roman civilization running from roughly AD 300 to 650; it is the foundational epoch for the visual language of iconography and for Christian culture in general.

Latria (from Greek *adoration*): The worship of adoration offered to God alone, for His own sake, because He is all Good in Himself. Contrast: *dulia*.

Lorica (from Latin *armor*): Any of several types of Roman armor.

Loros: The jeweled stole originally worn by Eastern Roman emperors, often appearing in iconography around Cosmos, royal figures, and occasionally angels.

Magus (plural *magi*): A practitioner of certain Near Eastern religions and esoteric disciplines, such as astrology and fortune-telling. The most famous magi are those who paid homage to the newborn Christ.

Mandorla (from Italian *almond*): A type of *aureole* that emanates from the whole body of a holy person. Mandorlas frequently represent the breaking-in of the heavenly sphere into our world.

Mantiya (from Slavonic *mantle*): The liturgical mantle worn by bishops and certain monastics.

Manus Dei (from Latin *hand of God*): Usually seen inside of or reaching out from the *Arc of Heaven*. The hand is often seen blessing saints, crowning kings, and performing other actions of divine approbation.

Maphorion (plural *maphoria*): The hooded cloak worn by the Mother of God and many other women in iconography. In the Slavic tradition, often called an *omophorion*.

Menaion (from Greek *of the month*): The fixed cycle of daily liturgical commemorations. Also, the book used for these celebrations.

Merilo (from Slavonic *measure*): A rod held by angels as a symbol of their duties as messengers and in reference to the measure used by them in Apocalypse.

Mystagogy (from Greek *initiation into mysteries*): The process by which prayer—especially the Divine Liturgy, the Holy Mysteries, and the use of sacramentals such as icons—works to imbue the worshipper with a mystical understanding of the Holy Religion.

Mysterion (from Greek *secret*): A sacred truth or rite, especially the Holy Mysteries of the Church. In the latter definition, it is synonymous with *sacrament*, though perhaps with a slightly different connotation.

Narthex (from Greek *scourge whip*): The vestibule at the western end of the church, to which in former times catechumens and penitents were dismissed prior to the Creed. The Greek root word relates to the corporal penance formerly performed by penitents.

Nave (from Latin *ship*): The central portion of the church, where the laity experience the Divine Liturgy.

Nimbus (from Latin *cloud*; plural *nimbi*): A type of *aureole* that emanates from the head of a holy person. Also called a *halo*, though floating three-dimensional discs that are not nimbi are in other art styles also called haloes.

Nimbus, Cruciform: A nimbus, usually on Christ, bearing the shape of the cross behind the head; it represents the Trinity. Also called a *nimbus cruciger*.

Omophorion (from Greek *shoulder carry*; plural, *omophoria*): The long, wide band of fabric worn around the shoulders by a bishop as a symbol of his authority. Also, in the Slavic tradition, another name for the Mother of God's *maphorion*.

Orarion: The long, narrow band of fabric worn around the shoulders by deacons and subdeacons as a symbol of their Holy Orders.

Orans (from Latin *praying*): A formal prayer posture with palms upward and usually to one's sides, though occasionally forward; it derives from the common human instinct to place one's palms up-and-out when pleading with someone. Used by most religions of the classical Roman world.

Orbiculum (from Latin *small orb*): An ornate patch of rank or decoration that was removable so that a new patch could be added or an old patch could be moved to a new garment. Also called a *segmentum*.

Pantocrator (from Greek *ruler of all*): An *epithet* of Christ. See icon entry.

Personification: A representation of a concept or a non-living thing as a human person in order to make its qualities more manifest. One example in iconography is *Jordan*. Another example from modern times is Uncle Sam, who signifies the United States.

Phiro: A skullcap worn by bishops.

Platytera Ton Ouranon (from Greek *more spacious than the heavens*): An *epithet* of Mary. See icon entry.

Pectoral Cross: A large cross worn by bishops around the neck as a symbol of office. Also called an *encolpion*.

Pendentives: The four, usually triangular, supports of a dome.

Phelonion (from Greek *cloak*)**:** The outer, poncho-like liturgical garment worn mostly by priests but also occasionally by bishops.

Proskynesis (from Greek *kissing toward*)**:** The profound bow of deepest adoration.

Prothesis (from Greek *setting forth*)**:** The Liturgy of Preparation performed quietly before the Divine Liturgy. Also, the small table on the northern wall of the sanctuary on which the Liturgy of Preparation occurs. Also known as the *Table of Oblation*.

Protomartyr (from Greek *first martyr*)**:** An *epithet* of St. Stephen.

Reverse Perspective: Depicting things that are farther away as larger than things that are nearer, so that the vanishing point is not on the horizon but inside the viewer. Through this technique, icons seem to leap out from themselves. Also called *inverse perspective*. It is contrasted with linear perspective, which creates a normal three-dimensional effect, such as is common in modern Western art.

Ripidion: A liturgical fan, similar to a cherubim's wing, used during the Eucharistic prayers.

Riza (from Slavonic *robe*)**:** A metal layer attached to an icon; usually pressed to resemble what it covers and typically leaving only the face, hands, and feet exposed. Also called an *ohklad*.

Romaion (from Greek *Roman*; plural *Romaioi*)**:** The name by which the Greek-speaking subjects of the Eastern Roman Empire called themselves, even after the fall of the Western Empire in AD 476. The civilization based in Constantinople was still the *Basileia Romaion*, the Empire of the Romans. The wholly unauthentic term "Byzantine" was invented after the fall of the empire by hostile historians who wished to deemphasize its connection to classical Rome and Greece.

Romanitas (from Latin *Roman-ness*)**:** The qualities and universal character of Christian Roman civilization, especially of its two primary components, the Greek and Latin cultures. Not to be confused with or narrowed down to Latin-ness. Iconography's universality derives in large part from its *Romanitas*.

Rotulus (from Latin *small wheel*)**:** Similar to a scroll, except that it only winds up on one pole and tends to be much longer. Typically used for public records and other information that did not need to be regularly referenced.

Royal Doors: The two central doors of the iconostasis, usually reserved for clergy. Also called the *Holy Doors*.

Sakkos (from Greek *sack-cloth*)**:** A tunic worn by bishops that symbolizes the robes worn by Christ during His Passion, and that therefore also symbolizes His suffering.

Saltire Cross: An X-shaped cross, such as the one on which St. Andrew was crucified and which has become his attribute.

Sanctuary: The sacred space behind the iconostasis where the Holy Mystery of the Eucharist takes place.

Septuagint (from Latin *of the seventy*): The original Greek translation of the Old Testament done by seventy-two elders of Israel circa 200 BC. It was based on original Hebrew texts now lost to history. It was the common version used by Greek-speaking Jews around the time of Christ and by the Greek Church Fathers, and it is the traditional source text for the Greek and Slavic churches. In the New Testament, two-thirds of the Old Testament quotes are from the Septuagint version, including most of the passages quoted by Christ Himself. Its name is often abbreviated *LXX* from the Latin for "seventy."

Shadows: Not typically depicted. In iconography, unlike in realistic schools of art, light emanates *from* the icon, as it is a window into the perfect world of Light beyond this one. Thus, light is not depicted as being cast from some outside source *onto* objects in an earthly fashion. For this same reason, there are no depictions of atmospheric effects, and distant objects in the background are not blurred to simulate our difficulty seeing far-away objects.

Simultaneous Narration: See *condensed time*.

Sticharion: The basic liturgical robe common to all orders of clergy.

Sticheron (from Greek *versicle*): A specific type of hymn used during liturgies.

Superhumeral (from Latin *above the shoulders*): A jeweled neck mantle, originally worn in the imperial court of Constantinople and seen occasionally on angels in iconography.

Suppadaneum (from Latin *under the feet*): The footrest on Christ's cross, represented by the third bar on a three-bar cross.

Synaxis (from Greek *gathering*): A secondary feast day after a primary feast day, to commemorate a particular saint involved in the primary feast.

Synoptic Gospels (*synoptic* from Greek *general view*): The Gospels of Matthew, Mark, and Luke, which are similar in style and content and markedly different from John's Gospel.

Tallit (from Aramaic *cover*): A Jewish prayer shawl, usually white with blue trim.

Temple (from Latin *shrine* or *sacred space*): The more accurate way to refer to the parish's worship building, particularly in the Greek Rite. The word "church" most exactly means the people of the parish.

Tetragrammaton (from Greek *four letters*): The name of God in the Old Testament—*YHWH*, that is, *Yahweh*, often translated *I Am Who Am*. It is usually written as *Lord* in English Bibles.

Tetrapod (from Greek *four foot*): The small table near the east end of the nave, where the faithful can venerate icons and the blessings of objects take place.

Theotokos (from Greek *God-bearer*): A title of Mary that emphasizes her role as true and fleshly mother of God; infallibly defined by the Council of Ephesus in AD 341.

Theosis (from Greek *become God*): The process by which the soul comes to participate in the divine nature. Prayer before and contemplation of icons may assist this.

Titulus (from Latin *title*): The title plate of an icon.

Titulus Crucis: The title of Christ on which was written "Jesus of Nazareth, King of the Jews" in Greek, Latin, and Hebrew; it was fixed to the upper portion of His cross and is signified by the small top bar on a three-bar cross.

Troparion (from Greek *something repeated*; plural *troparia*): A short liturgical hymn relating to the feast or saint of the day. Often called a *tropar*, plural *tropari*, in churches of Slavic tradition.

Type (from Greek *mark*): A person, thing, or event in the Old Testament that prefigures Christ, His Church, or something else directly related to Christ, such as the Virgin Mary. Examples include Moses' outstretched arms, which foreshadowed Christ on the cross, and Jonas' three days in the whale, which signify Christ's three days in the tomb.

Vault (from Old French *turn*): The semi-cylindrical ceiling of the nave of a church; the ceiling of St. Nicholas Church is a vault, or more specifically, a barrel vault. Contrast: *dome.*

Visual Shorthand: An item included in an icon, often in abstracted form, to concisely convey a specific meaning. For example, a simplified Temple of Jerusalem will frequently appear in the background to inform the viewer that the scene takes place in the holy city.

Wimple: A popular medieval ladies' garment covering the head and neck.

Worship (from Old English *worthiness*): An English word that formerly meant veneration, reverence, or adoration. As a result of confusion experienced by some Christians regarding the different types of worship, modern usage typically confines this word to adoration. See also *dulia, hyperdulia,* and *latria.*

Appendix VIII: Index

of driving away, 127
of fear, 81, 104, 106
of gratitude, 99
of indication, 3, 21, 93, 117, 135
of love, 137
orans, 6
of reaching, 104, 138
of sorrow, 74, 79, 133
of supplication, 6, 29, 93, 118
of testing, 92
veiled for reverence, 71-72, 77-79, 92-93, 112, 114

Globes, 18

Globus, 9, 18, 25, 59
cruciger, 18, 59

Glossolalia, 85

God, 4-10, 13, 17-18, 21, 24-25, 27, 29, 31-32, 35, 37-41, 43-45, 50, 52, 65-68, 70, 72-80, 84-85, 89-95, 100-101, 103, 106, 109-112, 114-115, 117, 120-121, 123-125, 127-128, 133-135, 137-139
Lamb of , 78, 92, 128

God-man, 73, 74, 80, 94, 99, 109, 111, 134

Gold (metal), 29, 71, 90, 92, 96

Golgotha, 66, 79, 80, 82, 133

Gospels, 10, 21, 27, 30, 32, 36, 50, 80, 82, 85, 91-92, 96, 101, 104, 114, 124-125, 134-135, 138

Gospel of Nicodemus, 134-135, 138

Gospel of Pseudo-Matthew, 91

Grace, 4, 8, 13, 27, 44, 72, 80, 81, 94, 110, 111, 117, 138

Great Entrance, 17, 125

Greece, 7

Greek,
alphabet, 6, 10
Catholic Church, 56, 61
Koine dialect, 30
language, 3, 4, 5, 6, 7, 9, 10, 20, 21, 30, 31, 39, 54, 56, 68, 85, 92, 93, 104, 133, 134, 137, 144
Rite, 4, 27, 31, 52, 56, 59, 100

Hades (place or state), 79-80, 114, 123, 135, 137-139
personification of, 138-139

Hagia Sophia, 56

Halo, 4, see also: Nimbus

Handmaiden of the Lord, 7, 67, 72

Hands, 3, 6-7, 9-10, 13, 18, 21, 23, 25, 27, 29, 31, 38, 40, 42, 44, 50, 71, 72-74, 77-79, 92-93, 104, 106, 109, 112, 114, 117-118, 120-121, 124, 127, 131, 133-134, 137

Hand of God (depiction), 13

Head, 4, 8, 10, 20, 24-25, 27, 35-36, 52, 59, 68, 96, 101, 118, 133-135

Heart, 42, 96, 101, 104, 106

Heaven(s), 4-6, 8, 10, 13, 17, 21, 24, 35-36, 39-40, 43, 45, 52, 66, 72-75, 81, 83, 85, 89, 93-94, 100-101, 106, 110, 117, 123, 134-135, 143

Hebrews, 3, 4, 5, 8, 9, 13, 30, 33, 38, 45, 59, 80, 96, 111, 120, 133, 144

Hell, 92, 134, 137-138

Henoch the patriarch, 43

Heresy, Arian, 50

Herod I, 90

Hierarchy,
Ukrainian Catholic, 61
visual, 134

Hierarchical perspective, 5, 6, 13, 24, 90

Hierotheus (bishop), 76

Himation, 4, 10, 13, 20, 25, 127

History, 32, 65-68, 100, 103, 110

Holiness, 29, 41, 71, 80, 82, 94, 96, 109, 118, 137

Holy Eucharist, see: Eucharist

Holy Family (the), 21

Holy Mysteries, 21, 27, 29, 36, 65, 94, 100, 131, 134

Holy Spirit, Holy Ghost, 4, 6, 10, 20, 27, 36, 65-66, 72, 80, 83-85, 93-94, 104, 110-111, 143

Hosanna(s), 123, 127

Hoshen, 96

Host(s), 8, 40, 75, 91, 93

Human, 5, 7, 9, 20, 38, 41-42, 60, 68, 70, 73, 76, 80, 82, 89, 99-100, 110-112, 114

Humility, 72, 124

Hyperdulia, 112

IC XC, 7, 60

Icon(s), 3-6, 8, 10, 13, 17-18, 20-21, 23-24, 27, 37, 50, 56, 61, 65-68, 71, 73, 77, 80, 82, 84-85, 89, 92, 99-101, 104, 106-107, 110-112, 115, 120, 123-124, 131, 133-135, 138-139, 142

Icon screen, see: Iconostasis

Iconoclasm, 112

Iconodulia, 111

Iconographer(s), 7, 18, 21, 23-24, 29, 36, 71, 95, 96, 99, 107

Iconography, 5, 7, 10, 33, 59, 68, 70, 92, 104, 123, 144

Iconostasis (Iconostases), 17, 18, 25, 27, 111

Ignatius (Russian Orthodox Patriarch), 58

IHS, 54

Image of Edessa, 33

Incarnate Logos, 7

Incarnation, 8, 73

Incense, 27, 29, 125

Inconsistent perspective, 123

India, 31

Isaac, 92, 104

Isaias, 6, 8, 13, 37, 40, 75, 86, 91, 95, 128

Islam, 52

Israel, Israelites, 8, 13, 27, 33, 35, 41, 42, 43, 45, 70, 76, 77, 86, 91, 92, 95, 96, 101, 110, 111, 124, 127, 128, 131, 138, 143
New, 42, 45, 107, 128

Jacob, 30, 72, 76, 104
in the etymology of "James," 30

Jacob's Well, 103-104

James of Alphaeus, 25, 34, 79, 82

James of Zebedee, 24-25, 30, 34, 109

Jeremias the prophet, 37-38, 45, 128

Jericho, 118, 120, 121

Jerusalem, 17, 23, 34, 38, 41, 44, 45, 52, 56, 59, 65, 73, 75, 77, 80, 83, 95, 99, 103, 104, 109, 115, 123, 125, 133
New (heaven), 17
Temple of, 6, 17, 23, 27, 41, 56, 70-71, 73, 77, 99-100, 117, 123, 127-128, 133
walls of, 80

Jesse, 13
rod / root of, 13, 120
Tree, 104

Jesus Christ, 3-10, 13, 17-18, 20-21, 23-25, 27, 29-37, 33-35, 40, 42-44, 54, 60, 66-68, 70, 72-82, 84-86, 89-96, 99-101, 103-104, 106-107, 109-112, 114-115, 117-118, 120-121, 123-125, 127-128, 131, 133-135, 137-139, 143, see also: Son of God
the Bridegroom, 99-100
Child, 7-8, 21, 77, 90-91
Conquers, 60, 65
Emmanuel, 8, 21
the Eternal High Priest, 103
Eucharistic, 32, 107
etymology of the title, 5
in Glory, 21, 74-75, 78
the God-Man, 111
the Incarnate Logos, 7
the King, 17, 42, 92, 123-124
the Lamb of God, 78, 92, 128
the Light, 82, 91, 109-111

the Messiah, 5, 13, 38, 45, 92-93, 124
miraculous image of, 33
the New Wine, 100-101
as a rabbi, 20, 35, 109, 115, 118
Son of David, 121, 123-124
Son of God, 4, 10, 21, 35, 50, 72, 75, 79, 90, 93-94, 100, 109-110, 112, 114, 120-121, 124, 134-135, 137
Sun of Justice, 4
the Way, 36
as Holy Wisdom, 56
Word of God, 7, 10, 27, 84

Jews, 35, 44, 80, 83, 84, 91, 92, 95, 103, 112, 118, 120, 133, 135

Jezabel, 43

Joachim, 67, 70

Joanna, 81, 82

Joel the prophet, 84

John the Baptist, see: John the Forerunner

John the Theologian, 10, 12-13, 23, 30, 32, 36, 74, 79-80, 101, 109, 131, 133-135

John the Forerunner, 8, 31, 43, 71, 93-96, 111, 137-138

Jonas the prophet, 37

Jordan River, 93-96

Josaphat, see: Kuntsevych, Josaphat

Joseph the Betrothed, 67, 70, 77, 89, 91, 128, 137, 138

Joseph of Arimathea, 79-80

Joseph's doves, 78

Josue of Nun, 95

Juda(h), see also: Judea
etymology of "Jude," 33
Kingdom of, 38, 42, 45

Judas Iscariot, 23, 24, 33, 76, 89, 103, 107, 123, 124, 125, 131, 133

Jude Thaddeus, 25, 33

Judea, Judeans, 35, 44, 84, 71, 143, see also: Juda

Judgment, 3, 68, 86, 138

Judith, Book of, 69

Justin Martyr, 91

Justinian I the Great, 56

Kekryphalos, 7, 71

Kings, 3, 6, 8, 17, 35, 37, 41-44, 59, 75, 89-92, 111, 123-125, 133-134, 138-139
Cosmos, 83
of Babylon, 44
of Edessa, 33
Generic, 35, 71, 75, 125
of Israel, Juda, or Judea, 37, 40, 42, 43, 89, 90, 111, 124, 138
Magi, 92
of Poland, 59

Kingdom, 41, 72, 74, 100, 106, 117, 123-124, 133, 135

Kingship of Christ, 4, 92

Kuntsevych, Josaphat, 58

Kyiv, 52, 61

Kyivan Rus', 144

Labarum, 54

Lacerna, 25

Lamb of God, 29, 78, 92, 128, 135

Lambs, 77, 92, 127, 128

Lamentations, Book of, 38

Last Supper, see: Mystical Supper

Late Antiquity, see: Antiquity

Latin,
Church, 52, 54, 59
dress, 25
language, 9, 30, 80, 133

Latria, 112

Law, see: New Law, Old Law

Lazarus, 82, 89, 112, 114-115, 124, 138

Lent, Great, 84

Levites, 27

Libya, 84

Licinius I, 54

Light, 4, 20, 77, 89, 95, 104, 115, 137
   of God, 4, 8, 13, 109-111, 137, 139
   held by maidens in the Temple, 70
   Christ our, 82, 91

Liturgy, 3, 6, 17, 18, 21, 25, 29, 32, 34, 40, 52,
   60, 65, 67, 75, 109, 125, 135, see also: Divine
   Liturgy
   Catholic, 125
   celestial, 29
   of Preparation, 135

Loaves, 23, 78, 104, 107, 131

Loaves of Proposition, 77-78, 131

Logos, Incarnate, 7

Longinus, 96, 135

Lorica squamata, 96

Loros, 84

Love, 32, 66, 75, 78, 99-100, 112, 128, 135, 137

Lubachivsky, Myroslav Ivan, 61

Luke the Evangelist, 10, 12, 13, 21, 36

Lycia, 50

Machabees, Books of, 69

Machabeus, Simon, 124

Madian, 104

Magi, see: Magus

Magisterium, 20

Magus, 92

Malachias the prophet, 95

Man, 5, 17, 20, 21, 67, 80, 85, 94, 128

Mandorla, 8, 74, 109, 137

Mandylion, 33

Manger, 89-91, 114

Manna, 101

Mantiya, 59

Manus Dei, see: Hand of God

Maphorion, 7, 21, 50, 133

Mark the Evangelist, 10-11, 13, 36

Marriage, 5, 67, 99, 100, 101

Martha of Bethany, 82, 112, 114

Martyrs, 27, 31, 32, 58-59, 104, 135

Mary the Mother of God, 7-8, 21, 49-50, 65-75,
   77, 79, 81-82, 90-91, 99-100, 111-112, 133,
   135

Mary Magdalene, 79, 81-82, 133

Mary of Bethany, 82, 112, 114, 124-125

Mary of Cleopas, 79, 81-82, 133

Master, 13, 20, 23, 93, 120, 124

Matthew the Evangelist, 10, 11, 13, 24, 25, 35,
   36,
   as Levi, 35

Matthias the Apostle, 33, 76

Maxentius (emperor), 54

Medallion, 6, 8

Medes, 84

Mediterranean, 18, 101, 124

Merchants, 127

Mercy, 24, 35, 42, 109-110, 121, 123, 134-135,
   144

Merilo, 9

Mesopotamia, 84

Screen (icon), see: Iconostasis

Scribes, 10, 96, 123, 127-128

Scriptures, 6, 20, 27, 30, 35, 43, 68, 74, 82, 92, 96, 106, 114, 134

Scrolls, 10, 37, 83, 84, see also: Rotulus

Seasons, liturgical, 65

Sembratovych, Sylvester, 61

Sephora, 104

Seraphim, 40, 74, 75

Seven (number in the Bible), 10, 27, 41, 56, 131

Sheep, 45, 134

Shepherd(s), 89, 91-92

Sheptytsky, Andrei, 61

Shield(s), 25, 54, 96, 135

Sichar, 104

Sidonian, 43

Signs, 27, 37, 44

Siloam, Pool of, 115

Simeon the God-Receiver, 66, 77, 78

Simon the Zealot, 25, 34, 101

Simultaneous narration, 90, 99, 115, 120, 121, 133, see also: Condensed time

Sin, 13, 23, 34, 40, 42, 60, 67, 75, 78, 80, 83, 91, 94-95, 100, 114-115, 127-128, 135, 137

Slavs, 50, 124

Slipyj, Josyf, 61

Smotritsky, Meletius, 59

Soldier, 25, 96, 135

Solomon, 6, 37, 41-42, 56, 137-138

Son of God, 4, 10, 21, 35, 50, 72, 75, 79, 90, 93-94, 100, 109-110, 112, 114, 120-121, 124, 134-135, 137

Souls, 5, 27, 34, 74, 75, 77, 79, 90, 107, 114, 123, 134, 139

Soviets, 61

Spirit(s), 5, 96, 103, 106, 117, see also: Holy Spirit

Star(s), 7-8, 89, 90, 92

Stephen the Protomartyr, 10, 17, 27, 28

Sterniuk, Volodymyr, 61

Sticharion, 27

Students, 13, 20, 117

Sun, 4, 8, 81

Superhumerals, 9

Suppadaneum, 79

Susanna, 82

Sviatoslav I of Kiev, 52

Swaddling clothes, 74, 89, 90, 114

Sycamore tree, 118, 120

Symbol, 9, 37, 43, 54, 58-60, 67, 78, 94, 124

Synod of Lviv, 61

Synoptic Gospels, 10

Syria, Syrians, 7, 110

Tabernacle(s), 27, 78, 109-110

Table, 23, 25, 27, 56, 99, 125, 127-128, 131, 135, 142

Tablets of the Law, 71, 111

Tabor, Mount, 109, 111

Tallit, see: Prayer shawl

Tax collector, 35, 96

Taxes, 118

Teachers, 10, 13, 18, 20, 103, 117, 124

Western Sacred Art, see: Sacred Art, Western

Wheat, 18, 138

Widows, 118

Wimple, 52

Wind, 20, 83, 104, 106

Wine, 18, 23, 25, 99-101, 125, 131

Wisdom, 7- 8, 10, 13, 18, 27, 33, 41-42, 44, 50,
    56, 67, 76, 118, 134
    Book of, 69
    Holy, 56

Word, Word of God, 7, 10, 27, 84

World (the earth; the current age), 8, 20, 34, 43,
    60, 74-76, 80, 84, 90-91, 110-112, 115, 118,
    125, 137
    ancient, 4, 59, 124
    the other, 109

Worship, 29, 41, 44, 67, 92, 100, 111, 112, 120,
    127, 128, 131, see also: Dulia, Hyperdulia,
    Latria

Xenolalia, 85-86

Yaroslav I the Wise, 56

YHWH, 4, 96, 111

Zacharias, 8, 70-71, 123

Zacheus, 118, 120

Zelomi, 92

Zoroastrianism, 92

About Leonine Publishers

Leonine Publishers LLC makes fine Catholic literature available to Catholics throughout the English-speaking world. Leonine Publishers offers an innovative "hybrid" approach to book publication that helps authors as well as readers. Please visit our web site at www.leoninepublishers.com to learn more about us. Browse our online bookstore to find more solid Catholic titles to uplift, challenge, and inspire.

Our patron and namesake is Pope Leo XIII, a prudent, yet uncompromising pope during the stormy years at the close of the 19th century. Please join us as we ask his intercession for our family of readers and authors.

Do you have a book inside you? Visit our web site today. Leonine Publishers accepts manuscripts from Catholic authors like you. If your book is selected for publication, you will have an active part in the production process. This book is an example of our growing selection of literature for the busy Catholic reader of the 21st century.

www.leoninepublishers.com